I0023703

When Out Isn't An Option

Marriage Should be for Keeps

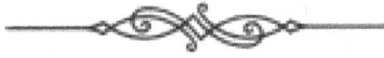

By Adriene Conner

BK
ROYSTON
Publishing

BK Royston Publishing
http://www.bkroystonpublishing.com
bkroystonpublishing@gmail.com

© Copyright – 2023

All Rights Reserved. No part of this book may be reproduced, stored in a retrieval system, or transmitted by any means without the written permission of the author.

Amplified Bible (AMP) Copyright © 2015 by The Lockman Foundation, La Habra, CA 90631. All rights reserved.
English Standard Version (ESV) - The Holy Bible, English Standard Version. ESV® Text Edition: 2016. Copyright © 2001 by Crossway Bibles, a publishing ministry of Good News Publishers.
King James Version (KJV) – Public Domain
The Message (MSG) - Copyright © 1993, 2002, 2018 by Eugene H. Peterson
New International Version (NIV) - Holy Bible, New International Version®, NIV® Copyright ©1973, 1978, 1984, 2011 by Biblica, Inc.® Used by permission. All rights reserved worldwide.

Cover Design: Sam Art Studio

ISBN-13: 978-1-959543-24-4

Printed in the United States of America

Dedication

I dedicate this book to every married couple who desperately desire to beat the marriage statistics, while enjoying a healthy and happy marriage.

It is also dedicated to those who are in serious relationships with a strong desire to someday enter into a marriage covenant.

Lastly, "When Out Isn't An Option" is dedicated to those who have already gone through the painful process of divorce, but still hold on to the dreams of having another opportunity to be involved in an intimate and loving marriage!

Acknowledgements

First and foremost, I would like to acknowledge Jesus Christ, who is my Lord and Savior. I am thankful and beyond grateful how God has afforded me the opportunity to live a life that overflows with peace, joy, and abundance as I continue to seek His face.

I want to thank my wonderful husband Elder Shawn Conner, who has allowed me the time and space to bring this book to fruition. Thank you for staying by my side for over thirty one years. Though this union hasn't always been easy, you continue to love me more today than when we first said "I do." You are my husband, companion, friend, and my prayer partner. You have always supported me in all of life's endeavors, even when those endeavors didn't work out the way I prayed they would work. I'm so thankful and grateful to God how you have always provided for our family. God has used you to make my life this side of heaven so much more pleasurable. My life has been made better and more enjoyable because of you. I love you with all of my heart!

I want to thank my two sons Caleb Conner and Joshua Conner whom I love with everything within me. Parenting the two of you didn't come with a handbook that provided us with all the rules and intricate details of parenting. If it did, we didn't get a copy. Despite all of our mix-ups and mess-ups, you two continued to love us through it all. As parents, though we didn't get it all right, you continue to give us the space for grace. I am proud of you guys in so many ways and I love you dearly! May God forever bless and keep you!

I would also like thank my Mother who is one of my greatest supporters. I also thank God for my family and friends who God has surrounded me with, who have like-kindred spirits. You ladies and gentlemen love the Lord with all of your hearts. You are strong in faith. I'm grateful how God has so graciously used each of you to push me when I needed to be pushed. You have encouraged me, cried with me and have been my support throughout this Christian journey. You know who you are. You Guys Rock!

Table of Contents

INTRODUCTION

"When Out Isn't An Option" is a book as well as a self-help guide, that was written to all couples who are in serious relationships. More importantly, it's written to individuals who are in a marriage covenant, who sometimes find marriage to be a gut-wrenching experience. Although marriage is instituted by God and yields amazing fruits with wonderful benefits attached, the process of becoming one is a life-long process that is bitter-sweet. The process of becoming one will call for the couple to die totally to themselves in order for the marriage and the relationship to live.

The book that you hold was inspired and written due to a deep God-given desire I had to be a blessing to relationships. I was determined that I no longer wanted to hide my pain, but I wanted all the pain of my past to be able to help others in their present as well as their future. I had a deep desire to pull the covers back in our marriage for others to take a peek into how we made it and continues to make it over, from one challenge to the next challenge. I wanted the reader to know that relationships can last and they can survive if the couple is willing to roll up their sleeves and give themselves away.

I believe that it is imperative in relationships for us to stop accepting the things we believe we cannot change and start changing those things that we simply cannot accept. We must come to a place where we both know and understand that if one of us wins, we both win. But, if one of us loses, we both lose.

The process of change can be one of the hardest and most difficult things that a human can take on in life. However, change can never be considered change when we are not willing to change. I believe in order for individuals to change and to stop living in painful relationships, they must realize that the price they're paying to stay the same, far outweigh the cost and the price of change. Always remember that there is no such thing as a resurrection, without there being a death that has already taken place.

As you dive into the pages of this book, I wholeheartedly believe that change is inevitable and a better, more fulfilling relationship is on the way, if you willingly apply the principles of God's Word. I have discovered that we don't always have to learn from our own mistakes in life, but life is designed that we can learn from the mistakes and failures of others. Are you willing to go ALL IN? If your answer is yes, let's embark upon a journey!

AFTER YOU SAY 'I DO'

In the beginning, was the Word, and the Word was with God, and the Word was God. Whether we know it or not, God instituted marriage and orchestrated the union of a husband and a wife. And because God orchestrated the union of a man and a woman, He should be at the helm of every marriage, and He should be the one who is leading it and guiding it if it is going to be generously blessed. My God, what blessed marriages we would have if we would allow God to be in charge as He has always intended to be!

I am reminded of a ship that has set sail. How many of you have ever taken a cruise? I have been tremendously blessed to go on seven voyages, to be exact. I love them! One thing I would like to say concerning all seven cruises is that every one of them started with a particular destination in mind. I had never boarded the ship, not knowing the particulars about where I was heading. However, I remember one time we had to be rerouted due to a severe storm.

Nevertheless, before we left the cruise terminal, the captain had already checked the weather forecast. He already factored in the possibility of intense winds and tumultuous seas that might interrupt and hinder the journey. In other words, the ship's captain knew the exact destination where he wanted to go, and he was knowledgeable in getting us there despite the detour. He knew how long the voyage was going to take to arrive. Every captain has at their disposal what you call a helm. The helm is a small device that's used as a steering apparatus that is very instrumental and particularly important in steering the ship and keeping the boat on course. It is designed to provide a level of control to the entire vessel to protect those traveling to their intended destinations. Without the helm directing the ship, the ship is liable to end up anywhere. The boat can end up in a place different from the area it initially set out to travel. And that is precisely how marriage is when two people refuse to allow God to be in control. God must be in charge. God must be the captain of the ship. He is the helm that we must allow to steer our lives. We must settle it in our hearts and minds that we are willing to humble ourselves and let God be at the forefront of our marriage because He knows the path we should take.

Just like the captain who is responsible for overseeing the ship and factoring in the possibility of detours, God knows from the onset that every marriage journey will sustain heavy winds and rain from time to time. God always foresees those times when we will have marriage-threatening catastrophes. He knows that if we do not stay connected to Him through discipline and obedience, we are sure to travel down dead-end roads that we never intended nor desired to travel down. God also knows that when we, as a couple, refuse to allow Him to navigate our marriages, we can begin feeling like a ship that is lost at sea and no longer on the radar. In other words, when we decide that we want to go it alone and do not need or desire God to be in charge, we will find ourselves in a place of lack and in a difficult position. Our marriage will have arrived at a site that is unfamiliar to us and in an area full of uncertainty, thereby causing us to begin feeling lost and alone without God's direction. I want to encourage you here because my marriage has often been in that place of uncertainty. Even today, whenever my husband and I fall short of obeying the Word of God, which is the will of God, it's not a pretty picture. Falling short in a marriage is all a part of the growth process and a learning curve, but some things can be avoided. We can avoid hitting our heads against the wall to learn. I want my learning experiences to speak loudly to you so that you do not have to touch them to see if they are hot or not. I pray that you caught that. We can learn from having our own experiences, or we can learn from other people's experiences.

There have been many times in our marriage when our turning away from the leading of God's direction has caused us to suffer so much pain, yet so needlessly. We have experienced trying to go full speed ahead without allowing God to be in charge because of pride, anger, rebelliousness, and disobedience. We shipwrecked each time my husband and I tried to go it alone because we were too angry to obey God. *Hebrews 5:8 tells us that Jesus learned obedience from the things He suffered.* God, too, will allow us to learn obedience through suffering. Jesus had to suffer and learn obedience without one act of sin, but many times, we suffer and learn obedience because of sin. I believe we all know and have experienced how great that suffering can be and how devastating it is to our marriage. My friend, though I am not the perfect wife and I do not have the perfect marriage, I am learning more and more how to obey God. The reason I am learning to obey God is that the price of disobedience and rebelliousness is too great to pay, and the pain is too much to bear. I no longer want to suffer the consequences of blatantly operating in sin.

After we say, "I do," we should know that God has already placed reinforcements in our marriages. It does not matter how long you have been married. There is never a need to go and reinvent the wheel when it comes down to the Word of God. We must be willing to follow God's Word. Like Mary, when Jesus turned water into wine, Mary told the disciples, "Whatever He says to you, do it!" Whatever the Father says to you, could you do it? That is the only way that God will be able to be the captain in our marriages. God is so gracious, and He loves us so much. God gives us His Word so that we do not shipwreck. He gives us His Word, so our lives do not go off the rails.

I am reminded of when we went to the amusement park when I was much younger. Every amusement park had what they called bumper cars. How many of you remember the bumper cars? The bumper car ride was always one of my favorite rides. It was designed so that there would be no conceivable way for you to drive the car off the track. You would still be safe even if you hit someone else's car or ran into the side rails. And by chance, if you did run into someone else or hit the rails, your car would be out of service for a few seconds before you could get back on your journey of driving. The Word of God is the same way. It helps to protect us when we hit snags in the road. It helps to keep us safe. Yes, there will be times when we encounter some challenges and situations in which we may find ourselves inoperable for a moment, but if we get back on track in trusting God even in those times, God will put us back on the journey.

After we say, "I do," we must know that our marriage will always be under construction. And when we have this mindset that the union will always be under construction, it takes the pressure off us to think that we are married to a perfect human being. Never believe that God gave us our mates so that they can make all of our wildest dreams come true. Do not ever think that our mates are supposed to give our lives purpose and meaning that can only come from God. Never look to them to do only what God can do. When we look to our mates to play God, I believe that is a dangerous mindset that sends many marriages into a tailspin. That is way too much pressure to put on an imperfect human being. We must allow God to give us space for grace! My husband is not God, and I am not "Little Miss Wonderful!" I am always highly blessed when my husband comes alongside me and agrees with me in certain areas. It is beautiful to be in one accord. Married couples should be in one accord as much as lieth within them. But don't mistake that for thinking they are solely responsible for your happiness. We should go out of our way to make our mates happy, but never get to where we believe they are responsible for our peace and joy in the Holy Ghost. Can I tell you that there are places in me, needs, desires, and wants that I have that only God can fill and fulfill? God designed it that way, and I am glad that He did. Can we find anybody better at making the necessary repairs and adjustments to our marriages other than God? That answer is "no"!

We must learn how to go to God. We must learn how to depend upon God when our marriage is in trouble and in need of repair. Don't beat your mate down when things aren't going well or there is an apparent breakdown in your marriage. Go to God! I believe many of us, when our vehicles break down, we take our cars back to the original manufacturer. We take it back to the original dealer or someone specializing in automobile repairs. When we become ill, we go to the doctor, or we see a specialist. Many of us have even started to go online to take our health into our own hands. Thank God for the World Wide Web. When we are ill, we do not go to our best friend for a diagnosis or a prescription. We go to those whose specialty is in the area of illness we are experiencing. When we are hungry, we head to the kitchen, the supermarket, or our favorite restaurant. But, when our marriages need spiritual alignment, some of us run to everybody else before we run to the one who orchestrated marriage in the first place. If God created it, He knows how to keep it running smoothly. God knows how to fix what is broken and how to put it back together again, even after it has fallen completely apart.

Marriage — A Different Jurisdiction

Many years ago, my family and I traveled to Houston, Texas, to attend the home-going celebration of my mother's oldest sister. We were so anxious to arrive at our destination that my sister Pamelia was driving about 90 mph. The speed limit in New Orleans was 70 mph, and she was speeding. Back then, I would consider her to be a fast driver. We finally arrived at the Louisiana-Texas state line at about 9:00 p.m. While sitting in the back seat, I looked up in just enough time to see the sign that said, "Don't Mess with Texas. Buckle Up — It's the Law!" I am not sure why I always liked reading that sign.

Pamelia was tired of driving and asked if I was ready to take the wheel. I did. After I had been driving for about thirty minutes, Pamelia, dozing off in the back seat, lifted her head long enough to say to me, "Girl, you're driving like a snail. Step on it!" It was her vehicle. Therefore, I started speeding up with much apprehension, even though I was pretty skeptical about doing so. I pressed down on the accelerator, and before you knew it, I too, was going 90 mph. After several hours of driving, as I looked through the rear-view mirror, the only thing I could see in all that darkness behind me was flashing red and blue lights. Of course, it was the police! "Oh, my God, now I'm in trouble," I blurted out. Pamelia and everybody else in the back of the vehicle woke up quickly. My mom never went to sleep while driving on the road. She always said that if there was any chance of an accident taking place, she wanted to be awake to see what was happening. And she was pretty serious about that! So, after pulling over to the side of the road and showing the police officer the usual identifications, he wanted to know where we were going in such a hurry. "To my sister's funeral," my mom hastily said. The police officer said, "I am not going to give you a ticket, but slow down!" He then reminded me of what the speed limit was in Texas. I knew that speeding was speeding regardless of what state you are driving through at the time. I also learned that Louisiana and Texas had different speed limits. And, depending on where you are on the road, the speed limits are subject to change.

The highway speed limit differs from the speed limit while traveling through town.

I was born and raised in New Orleans, Louisiana. I traveled to Texas numerous times and found that Texas and Louisiana have a completely distinct set of laws that we must be governed by and willing to obey. The reason is that they are two states with two different jurisdictions, meaning they have a distinct set of rules. Therefore, what takes place in one state cannot be expected to take place in another state or another district.

Each state has its own set of rules in place. Consequently, when a couple decides to tie the knot, after saying "I do," they must make sure that they are not trying to live their married lives under the same rules that applied when they were single. After you say, "I do," you must realize that the same restrictions and conditions will no longer apply. I am talking about how you did things in your singleness, especially if you were single and incredibly independent for a long time before getting married. Learning how to live under different rules and guidelines was an area that was particularly hard for my husband and me to overcome. I am sure that it's hard for most couples. Not only was it difficult in the beginning stages of our marriage journey, but for many years into our marriage, we struggled significantly to realize that we were no longer single. We bumped heads more times than we care to remember or count. We soon came to realize that if we were going to survive, one or both of us had some seriously changing to do in order to stay married. We were in desperate need of some "Come-to-Jesus" moments. It should go without saying that marriage will always have those times when we must learn how to humble ourselves under the mighty hand of God!

We both were in our early twenties when we got married. Neither of us had been married before nor had children at the time. When we first met, Shawn was already a born-again believer in a backsliding position, and I was as lost as a ball in high weeds. I did not have a relationship with God as I thought I did, though I consulted Him on many occasions. To be straightforward, I was hopelessly lost without Christ on my side. All we knew was that we were in love and wanted to spend the rest of our lives together. We never factored in all the changes that had to be considered to have a blessed marriage. We were so green. It was not long before we realized that if our marriage was going to survive, we had to be willing to yield and submit our lives and marriage to the new captain in town. We desperately needed God to take the reins. We seriously needed God at the heart level amid all our love. Never get to a place in your marriage where you believe that love is enough or that it is sufficient in and of itself to help you to stand without God. We had to be willing to work on that sometimes-painful process of "becoming one" if we wanted peace and harmony in our marriage. We soon realized that many adjustments had to be made and are still being made to this day.

After you have traveled down those same dead-end roads, run through enough stop signs, and have seen enough caution signs in marriage, somewhere along the way, you learn how to do better. In *Isaiah 1:17*, God tells us to *"Learn to do well."* (KJV) When you're serious about marriage, you learn how to obey God and stop trying to live by the "Old Rules" of singleness because those rules no longer apply. You learn a little more about how to keep the doors closed to chaos and confusion at any cost because you learn that the cost of staying the same far outweighs the cost of changing. Likewise, the benefit of change is so much more rewarding that what we benefit from when we decide to stay the same. Think about that for a moment. In marriage, after you've said, "I do," you must be willing to embrace the stripping-away process and be ready to go into the fiery furnace that the real you can come forth. Pride will never allow the real you to emerge. A lack of humility will always prevent you from becoming the best version of yourself. God is always in the process of trying to strip away and burn up some things in our lives that are nothing more than a hindrance to our spiritual well-being. Ready or not, you must be willing to embark upon the journey of change for the good of the marriage and not be stuck in the interest of one. Selah!

The Process Of Becoming One

After you say, "I do," God tells us in His Word that the two shall become one flesh. That means, in the eyes of God, two individuals are to begin to function as one unit. When two become one, it is no longer about "Me, Myself, and I," but it now becomes "We." *Genesis 2:20 says, "And the man gave names to all the livestock, and to the birds of the air, and every animal of the field; but for Adam, there was not found a helper [that was] suitable (a companion) for him. (21) So the LORD God caused a deep sleep to fall upon Adam; while he slept, He took one of his ribs and closed up the flesh at that place. (22) And the rib which the LORD God had taken from the man He made (fashioned, formed) into a woman, and He brought her and presented her to the man. (23) Then Adam said, 'This is now bone of my bones, And flesh of my flesh; She shall be called Woman, Because she was taken out of Man.' (24) For this reason, a man shall leave his Father and his mother, and shall be joined to his wife; and they shall become one flesh."* (Amplified Bible)

After a couple gets married, God commands the man to leave his father and his mother and be joined to his wife. That means that God requires the relationship with parents, regardless of how loving they are, to no longer be permitted to take precedence or to supersede the relationship between the husband and the wife. The couple's children, family members, or friends must not come before the unbreakable bond that the husband and his wife should experience in the sight of God because they are one. The spouse comes first. Make sure you do not allow anyone to have an unhealthy position in your life regarding your marriage. God told the husband in *Genesis 2:24 to leave his parents and to cleave to his wife.* That means he is to stick close to her and vice versa. They are to be joined together as they cleave to one another. Couples pay a hefty price when they do not adhere to cleaving one to another.

Even though in the eyes of God, a married couple is considered one, remember that "becoming one" is a life-long process that must be continually worked on throughout the course of the marriage union. A couple should always be in the process of striving to become one — spiritually, emotionally, financially, and sexually. They should strive to have the same long-term goals for the health of their marriage. They should function as a team and continue travelling in the same direction regarding their marriage. As you live your lives as one, always keep it top of mind that you made a covenant vow to love and honor one another, and, more importantly, that you made a vow to God. And it is a vow that God takes very seriously, and it is one He intends for us to keep until death do us part.

I Die Daily

In every marriage, you can rest assured that there will be a dying process. No, I am not speaking about physical death but a spiritual one. And for those who are not willing to die spiritually, you might as well get ready to live a defeated life. In *1 Corinthians 15:31*, the Apostle Paul says, *"I die daily."* I would say that dying to self is one of the hardest things an individual can take on. I'm talking about born-again believers as well as non-born-again believers. We, by nature, are selfish individuals. That is why no one needs to teach a child to be selfish. Children, for the most part, are born selfish. Of course, there can be some exceptions to the rule. And when it comes down to crucifying the deeds of the flesh, it can be a daunting task. We do not have to feel hopeless in our attempts. We *can* put to death the deeds of our flesh. We *can* walk victoriously. I don't know about you, but I am so glad that the Lord does not leave us alone to take on life. I want to encourage you that all things are possible when we believe in God. I believe that the best thing we can do for our marriages is to die to ourselves. What exactly does that look like, someone may ask? Jesus tells us in *Luke 9:23*, *"...If [anyone would] come after me, let him deny himself, and take up his cross daily, and follow me."* (KJV, edited) Just like there could not be a resurrection without death first, it is impossible to experience life and life more abundantly without death first taking place in our lives. If you want God to breathe upon your marriage, and if you want it to be alive and vibrant, you must be willing to die. I will say it again. You must be willing to die to yourself daily. You cannot just sacrifice on Tuesdays and Thursdays and take the rest of the week off, but you must die every day. When we give our lives to the LORD, we are expected to relinquish our own will to God. We are no longer the boss that is in charge. We are no longer in charge of calling the shots. That scripture says that we must deny ourselves. I know that it's not anything that we willingly jump through hoops to do, but not denying ourselves will cause us to suffer, regardless of whether you see it or not. What I have discovered in life is that people are not eager to raise their hands and volunteer to go through a suffering process. There is no spiritual growth in life and marriage without suffering. When we take on suffering, we must endure to follow Jesus. Always remember that there is joy on the other side of the pain. God does not call us or expect us to suffer just for the sake of suffering. There is something that God has for us on the other side of that heartache. I can surely testify to that. I tell you, the place that God has brought my husband and me to, in these thirty-one years plus in our marriage, I would go through it all over again to get to where we are right now. We are not where we want to be, but I thank God every day that we are not where we used to be in our marriage. We have charted a course through a lot of rough terrain and territory to get to where we are right now. I want to pause right now and say, "To God be the Glory" for the things He has done! In a place of humility, I'd say that everybody wants a testimony without the test. There can be no testimony without first having to pass the test. Have you ever wondered why the word "test" is embedded within the word "testimony"? Not only must we be tested, but again, we must know how to pass the test. Troubles don't come to stay, but they "Come to pass." I realize that, sometimes, we have pop-up tests that show up in our lives just as they did when we were in school. Test and quizzes in our marriage can seem to come out of nowhere, but the Spirit of God will always help you to ace every test that shows up in your marriage when you trust God with your marriage. I want you to know that we will always be a student in the classroom of marriage. But again, don't get stuck in the process while the exam is taking place.

I am always curious about people who never come out of troubling times. They are always going through. *Luke 4:13* even tells us, *"When the devil had finished every temptation, he [temporarily] left Him until a more opportune time."* (Amplified Bible) This scripture tells us that there should be a season when you can breathe easily from the attacks from the enemy. God wants you to know, dear heart, that you cannot go on to *"Next"* until you can successfully master where you are right now. In school, we are passed to the next grade only when we have mastered the grade we were currently studying. And if we did not master the current grade, the teacher would keep us back so we can go over the material all over again until we have mastered the material, which really isn't a bad thing. In school, we are made to take the course all over again until we can pass the test. It's the same way in the kingdom of God when it comes down to marriage. Let's not keep repeating the test because we're not doing what it takes to pass the test. The way you master and overcome where you are right now is to be willing to die daily. Stay with me here because I'm still talking about what needs to happen after you say, "I do." I want you to know that you must be willing to allow a piece of you to die with every trial. Regardless of how bad your emotions are raging with every argument, the Spirit of God will still encourage you to die. Bad attitudes and short tempers must die. Trying to hold on to your right of being right must die. The spirit of selfishness and the what-about-me attitude must die. Every day, you will have at least one opportunity, if not more, to die so your marriage will live to see another day and to grow to another level. Stop trying to go to another level in your marriage without being willing to die to where you are right now. We would have never been able to celebrate the death, burial, and resurrection of Jesus Christ had Jesus never embraced the fact that He had to die in order for us to live. Somebody say "Hallelujah!" His death preceded us in having the ability to enjoy life and life more abundantly. Like Jesus, we must be willing to go to the cross and get through individual-death experiences, all with our focus on the other side. Go through the process keeping your eyes on the prize. The artists J.J. Hairston & Youthful Praise sing a song entitled "After This!" Can I encourage you to go through the process knowing there will be glory after this? Once you decide to die daily, know there will be victory after this. I am simply encouraging you to know that after you say "I do," you must be willing to die in the realm of the Spirit. I know that it is something that we do not like to talk about much, let alone willingly put into practice. But it's the truth, anyhow!

Walking in the Spirit

Having the willingness to die daily brings me to a fantastic promise that God gives us. *Galatians 5:14–16 says, "For the whole Law [concerning human relationships] is fulfilled in one precept, 'YOU SHALL LOVE YOUR NEIGHBOR AS*

YOURSELF' [that is, you shall have an unselfish concern for others and do things for their benefit]. (15) But if you bite and devour one another [in bickering and strife], watch out that you [along with your entire fellowship] are not consumed by one another. (16) But I say, walk habitually in the [Holy] Spirit [seek Him and be responsive to His guidance], and then you will certainly not carry out the desire of the sinful nature [which responds impulsively without regard for God and His precepts]. " (Amplified Bible)

What a tremendous promise that God has given us. In verse 16, God tells us that if we walk in the Spirit or be responsive to the Spirit's promptings, we will not be as fast to carry out the desires of our flesh. The flesh, which is our sinful nature, does not readily respond to God and the precepts of God. When we are led by the Spirit and act accordingly, that is how we learn how to die to ourselves daily. Walking in the Spirit is having the ability to hear God's voice and read God's Word and do exactly what He tells us to do. The Bible tells us the day that we hear God's voice, we must not harden our hearts. First and foremost, there is a danger in not hearing the voice of God. We must have the ability to hear the voice of God speaking to us as we go through our daily lives. When God tells us to "Walk in the Spirit," that means that we are putting His Word into practice every day. We must learn how to be obedient to God continually. The Amplified Bible says to do it "Habitually." In other words, make being obedient to the voice of God a daily lifestyle. Learn how to live under the influence of the Spirit of God. I promise you that when we walk in the Spirit daily, it becomes easier to see our marriage becoming a marriage that we can enjoy to the fullest and a marriage that glorifies our heavenly Father.

My sincere prayer for every married individual or couple who reads this book is that "After You Say I Do," regardless of how long you have been married, with every fiber of your being, you would protect the sanctity of your marriage. Marriage is truly a gift from God, and I pray you to see it as such. It is a gift that God desires for us to keep unwrapping so that we can continually enjoy the blessings, benefits, and fruit of a Godly marriage. It's a gift that we should be grateful for and one that we should always honor on this side of heaven!

PRESSING TOWARD THE MARK

In life, everything that is profitable, rewarding, significant, or meaningful for an individual to acquire will require you to press. Studying for a major exam will require a press. Earning a degree requires a press. Getting into the gym to lose or gain weight or to build muscle will require much discipline, and it too, will require a press. We all can agree that growing and maturing in God requires a press, and marriages are no different. If we desire a great marriage instead of a mediocre one, we'll have to learn how to press. The word press means to move into a position of contact with something by exerting continuous effort or physical force. Because we are speaking from a spiritual perspective here, in order to press in life and marriage, we must move into a position of contact with God by exerting continuous force in the realm of the Spirit. Say Amen!

To press means that you must be willing to apply some pressure, and you and I must be capable of standing during the process. It must be intentional when you think about pressing in the things of God. It must be done on purpose. It must be predetermined and carefully planned out. Nobody moves forward and gains ground in the realm of Spirit by accident. You do not haphazardly make it further up the road just by chance. While pressing, you must know that you will have to go against the odds to get the proper results in order to win. Despite every obstacle in our way, we must be adamant about applying continuous effort. Many times, when in the press, we'll have to know how to hope against hope while learning how to praise God anyhow.

Pressing not only requires much faith, but it also requires much focus. When all seems lost, pressing will require you to declare and decree, *"Lord, I believe, but help my unbelief,"* that I may continue to stand. When it comes down to marriage, I believe that when we are diligent about pressing, God will show us that those things that seem to be impossible are very much possible.

The Apostle Paul is one such person in the Word of God who knew how to press. He was a person amongst so many others who possessed great faith. And because of his faith, he was intentional and tenacious when it came down to his walk with God. Anybody who knows anything about him would know that he was once shipwrecked; he was thrown into prison several times, where some of the gospels were written from a prison cell. A viper bit him in Malta, but he still refused to lie down and die; he was stoned and dragged out of a city, left for dead, then got back up and went right back into that same city the next day to finish what God allowed him to start. Good God Almighty! He was struck blind by a light from heaven only to receive his sight three days later. All these things happened to him for the sake of the gospel.

A further study of the life of the Apostle Paul clearly shows that he had a great desperation about himself. His life not only shows us that he was desperate to know Christ, but he was desperate to be used by God. All he knew was that he wanted to win Christ, and he wanted to be found in Christ. The Bible tells us that he was zealous to gain Christ. The Apostle Paul was a tremendous trailblazer. I would say he was a spiritual giant in the things that pertained to God. What an incredible example that God has given us to show us what it means to press.

Pressing can be related to our walk with God in all areas of life as it pertains to our faith. Therefore, as you read, I want you to see how God wants you to press in your marriage to gain victory. Then, from this point forward, as you continue to navigate your way through this book, I want you to be fully aware that the pressing that is required of us in marriage and life is compared to being in a race on this Christian journey.

Marriage will cause us to press as we move forward in letting go of the past that has haunted our marriages for way too long. As married couples, we must let go of past hurts, pains, and failures if we desire to press. I believe that the only time and the only reason we should look back at our past hurts and faults is when God wishes to use our past to help others overcome those things that God has brought us through. Our misery can and is often used by God as we minister to others. We must realize that our present pain as well as our past pain and hurts can indeed help someone in the future. Right now, I have a business coach. I have heard him say many times, "We can help solve someone's problems simply because we used to be them." If you are not using your past to help somebody else in their deliverance, it is time to let go of the past and look ahead to what's before you. If your past is not benefitting you, or if it's not a steppingstone to your future, it's time to stop looking back. Can I pause right here to encourage you to use the pain of your past for the sole purpose of helping someone else? The enemy keeps many of us looking back so that we would be stagnated and unfruitful in life. I once heard a mighty woman of God say, "We cannot keep rehearsing our let-downs." We all experience let-downs in our marriage, but let-downs should be a vehicle for great come-backs. My friend, you must know that we will win more spiritual battles when we allow God's Word to be the final authority in our lives. We win more battles when we learn of the spiritual authority that God has given to every born-again believer.

I am speaking to those of you who desperately desire to gain Christ. I am talking to those of you who want to press toward the mark not only to be rewarded in this life, but to also look forward to a heavenly prize for pushing forward in the things of God. The Apostle Paul spoke about and looked for heavenly rewards because of his earthly press. So again, if you desire to gain wisdom, revelation, and spiritual insight from this book, you will have to take on the same mindset that the Apostle Paul had on his journey. He wasn't afraid to express to us what would be required of us to win in this race while on the path to destiny. God used his voice, which is still speaking so loudly to us to this day, to let us know that a press would be required if victory were to be had.

In the book of Philippians, the Apostle Paul was letting the church of Philippi know his life's goal. He wanted the believers to know that compared to all that he had accomplished, his distinguished background, and who he was up to the point of meeting Christ, none of it compared or measured up to the blessing of knowing Christ. The Apostle Paul said that those things that had been acquired and those things that were previously thought to be so great and so grand were worthless. He wanted us to know that there wasn't anything that could be compared to, equaled to, or even come close to growing in a deep relationship with Christ because this was a relationship that was incredibly priceless to him. I want to pick up reading in *Philippians 3:7, which says, "But whatever former things were gains to me [as I thought then], these things [once regarded as advancements in merit] I have come to consider as loss [absolutely worthless] for the sake of Christ [and the purpose which He has given my life]. (8) But more than that, I count everything as loss compared to the priceless privilege and supreme advantage of knowing Christ Jesus my Lord [and of growing more deeply and thoroughly acquainted with Him — a joy unequaled]. For His sake, I have lost everything, and I consider it all garbage, so that I may gain Christ, (9) and may be found in Him [believing and relying on Him], not having any righteousness of my own derived from [my obedience to] the Law and its rituals, but [possessing] that [genuine righteousness] which comes through faith in Christ, the righteousness which comes from God on the basis of faith. (10) And this, so that I may know Him [experientially, becoming more thoroughly acquainted with Him, understanding the remarkable wonders of His Person more completely] and [in that same way experience] the power of His resurrection [which overflows and is active in believers], and [that I may share] the fellowship of His sufferings, by being continually conformed [inwardly into His likeness even] to His death [dying as He did]; (11) so that I may attain to the resurrection [that will raise me] from the dead. (12) Not that I have already obtained it [this goal of being Christlike] or have already been made perfect, but I actively press on so that I may take hold of that [perfection] for which Christ Jesus took hold of me and made me His own. (13) Brothers and sisters, I do not consider that I have made it my own yet; but one thing I do: forgetting what lies behind and reaching to what lies ahead, (14) I press on toward the goal to win the [heavenly] prize of the upward call of God in Christ Jesus. (15) All of us who are mature [pursuing spiritual perfection] should have this attitude. And if in any respect you have a different attitude, that too God will make clear to you."* (Amplified Bible)

There is a lot to unpack and digest in these scriptures. The most important thing is that the Apostle Paul wanted to know Christ. If you look back at *Philippians 3:10*, you would read that he said, *"So that I may know Him."* He was speaking about knowing Christ in that particular text. The Apostle Paul was saying that he wanted to experience Him. He also said *"Becoming more thoroughly acquainted with Him."* He said he wanted to *"Experience the power of His resurrection,"* which overflows and the power that should be "Active in the lives of all believers." He didn't stop there. He said that he *wanted to* *"share the fellowship of his sufferings by being continually conformed inwardly."* And for that to take place, he knew he had to experience an inward death. The Apostle Paul knew that he had yet to arrive. He knew in order to take hold of that perfection or obtain what God had for him, his future could no longer be based upon or predicated upon his past. He knew that if he was going to move forward by faith, he could not hold on to past successes, nor could he keep on reminiscing and being reminded of all his past failures. It was imperative for him to leave all those things behind to press that he could win by gaining Christ.

The Flying Trapeze

How many of you have attended the circus? I used to love going to the circus as a young girl and a young adult. One of the most notable acts to me at the circus was the flying trapeze act. I was always fascinated by the fact that the participants had to know the exact time to let go of one person to make the connection with the person who was to catch them. And, if by chance they held on too long to the last person, they would miss connecting to the person who was before them, waiting to catch them. What a revelation! God can speak and give revelation just about through any situation.

I could remember God using this circus act to minister to me during a severe challenge my husband and I were having. God kept showing me that if I wanted to move forward in my marriage, I had to be willing to *"Let go"* of the past and what was behind me. He kept showing me in my anger that there was no way for me to move forward while simultaneously holding on to the chaos of the past. In other words, I had to move into a position of contact with Him by exerting some continual force in the realm of the Spirit if I wanted victory over my anger and emotions. On many occasions, He would flash a picture of the flying trapeze act before me to let me know that if I wanted to move on to the next thing in my life and in my marriage, I had to be willing to take some steps forward and not get consumed and paralyzed in the present situation.

Sometimes trials can have the capability to paralyze us if we allow them to do so. This is why the Apostle Paul said, *"This one thing that I do. I'm forgetting those things behind me, and I am reaching forth."* We must know how to let go if we want to gain ground and be victorious over our adversary, who is not our spouse-though sometimes we think and act as if they are. I want you to constantly be reminded that there will always be a forward reach in marriage. The Apostle Paul said he was *"reaching forward."* He was determined not to keep looking back because in this case, his looking back was only a hindrance to him. When we rebel against the Word of God by deciding that we don't want to *"Forget"* those things that come to kill, steal, and destroy our marriage and move forward, we must realize that we are just like the participant in the flying trapeze act who refuses to let go. When we refuse to let go of the traps and devices that the enemy sets, again, just like in the flying trapeze act, we will constantly go back and forth and do not get anywhere. You are going back and forward without making any real progress. We must make it our business to reach forward less there will be no conforming to the image of Christ Jesus. Remember, the Apostle Paul said that to conform, there must be an inward death. Again, he not only had to forget about his past successes to press forward, but he also had to forget about past failures. Again, we cannot keep on rehearing all of the let-downs associated with being married, lest there be no growth and no spiritual progress.

God is giving us that same invitation He offered and extended to the Apostle Paul. *Philippians 3:14* says, *"I press toward the mark for the prize of the high calling of God in Christ Jesus."* (Webster's Bible Translation)How many of you are willing to press toward the mark because you have a made-up mind that you want to reach the high calling of God in your life and your marriage? Always remember that God's high calling is an upward call to a more excellent way of living, but you and I must be willing to reach forward to obtain the greater and stop settling for the lesser.

When we reach, it means we are willing to stretch out in a specified direction to touch or grasp something. Therefore, if you want to touch God, that God may strengthen your marriage, you have to know what it is to reach past your own limitations and your own desires. You have to get beyond what is expected and what is ordinary. Ordinary can never be in the same class as greatness. It is mandatory that your faith be in an outstretched position. So, you must be willing, with the help of God, to press past your capabilities and stretch if you want to reach the high calling of God. I'm speaking to those who do not wish for their marriage to be another statistic.

The Apostle Paul was letting us know that he had not arrived, but he was on his way to something that was much better and greater than where he was. It was a press and a strain while he was in pursuit. And many times, to get to "The greater" in our marriage, you and I will have to strain sometimes, which means that we will have to put forth a strenuous and heroic effort to get there. I do not have to convince anybody who has been married for any length of time that marriage will always cause you to stretch. Don't be so surprised by the fact that stretching will cause you to also experience some agony along the way to victory. It's all a part of the growth process.

Rear-View Mirrors

Have you ever wondered why the manufacturer of vehicles purposely made the windows in front of the car much bigger than the rear-view mirrors? While driving, it is much more vital to keep our eyes on what is in front of us and where we are going instead of looking behind us and focusing on where we have been. The manufacturer knew that we would be seriously challenged in trying to drive and move forward in keeping our eyes on the road if most of our time and attention were being spent looking through the rear-view mirror. See, the rear-view mirror only shows us where we have been but does very little to show us where we are going. The rear-view mirror serves only as a precautionary measure designed to help us stay in our lanes while allowing us to navigate more smoothly while moving forward. I am sure that you get the idea. So, while trying to press in marriage, never let your past dictate or determine your future, until you are using it as a steppingstone to greater. It is a colossal mistake in marriages when we allow our past to suffocate, choke, and smother our future. Countless married couples find themselves stuck, broken down, and parked at the side of the road because they cannot let go of the past. The growth of their marriage has been stifled because they find it too hard to let go of yesterday. And because of such, they find it difficult, if not impossible, to move forward. Again, it is simply a trick of the enemy because we cannot simultaneously live in the past and progress toward the future. That's why the rear-view mirror was designed to be so small. Yet, the enemy has deceived so many couples because they're living their entire lives as married couples looking through the rear-view mirrors of life.

The Apostle Paul had the mindset that "I refuse to keep looking back. I refuse to allow my past to dictate my future." I once recall reading a quote in my Bible that the Spirit of God occasionally brings back to me when the adversary is working overtime to keep me looking back. The quote says, "It's hard to see your future when you keep staring at your past." I cannot tell you how many times I have had to meditate on that and how it has helped me on many occasions while trying to press in the things of God in my marriage and in life.

The enemy loves nothing better than our past to be a constant hindrance and roadblock to our future. I can also discern in the spirit that many of you find yourselves asking God to help you get over some things that have taken place in your past that you may press in order to reach forward. You are asking God to bring forth healing to help you to *get over it* so that you may be able to *go over it*. Many of you need healing from your past so that you may be able to go on to the next chapter in your life or even be able to turn the page. Some of you reading right now have been through some things in life that have left you traumatized, whether it came from your present spouse or someone else. And those things that have left you traumatized are now playing out in your current relationship and in your present marriage. It can be things like somebody who has touched you inappropriately, which keeps you looking through the rear-view mirror in your marriage. Someone who is reading right now, you were raped or molested as a child, a teenager, or as an adult, and it is such a hindrance that regardless of how much you try, it prevents you from looking forward. Somebody you so dearly loved with all your heart in a previous relationship or an earlier marriage has either divorced you or walked out on you, which keeps many of you looking back because you still find it a significant source of pain in your life. Somebody who meant the world to you has violated your trust in them, but can I tell you that God knows and God cares? God loves you so much.

Many of the things we have suffered in the past can and have become a severe roadblock in many marriages. They play a significant part, making it difficult for you to press. Most of them happened to you before you got married, and many during your marriage. They are still playing out in real-time in your marriage today. Many times, when people share traumatic experiences that have taken place in their lives either before marriage or even during their marriage, I encourage them to ask God to help them to press and to move forward one day at a time. We must remember that none of us are exempted from the trials and tribulations of life. We must know how to take life one day at a time because faith is only now. Yesterday is gone, and all we have is now because we cannot have confidence in tomorrow.

While I am not at the end of this particular chapter, I am led right now to pray for that individual or that couple whose past has been an obstacle to your future. I genuinely pray that you will receive the peace of God and that God will bind up and heal all of those open wounds you are currently experiencing in your marriage or relationship. I want to pray for the one who is greatly challenged in their efforts to press and to reach forward. I want to pray for the one who feels like, regardless of how long or how much you have tried to move forward, it feels like an elephant is sitting on you, keeping you stuck and stagnating in a holding pattern. So, right now, I declare and decree that by faith, this is the last day that your past will be used to suffocate you and to choke the life out of your future. I speak it into the atmosphere that you will no longer be hindered in your relationship and marriage. Your past will no longer keep you depressed. It will no longer hold you hostage to keep you down and out. Your past will no longer rob you of your peace and joy in the Holy Ghost. From this day forward, you will have the ability to reach forward and press toward the mark for the prize. I break every chain of bondage that has been sent to you to destroy you and your marriage because he whom the Son sets free is indeed free. I speak and say that the anointing of God, even now, will destroy every yoke of bondage. I speak and say that you are hopeful because of your future, and you are no longer hopeless and helpless because of your past. From this day forward, the only reason you will have to look back through your rear-view mirror is to see how far God has brought you on this Christian journey and in your marriage. From this day forward, the only reason you will look back and revisit your past is for God to help you with someone else's future. You will only look back and revisit your past when God is using your past to show them the power of God and what God can do in and through the life of an individual who is pressing and reaching forth. I declare and decree that your marriage is healed, healthy, whole, and strong in Jesus' name! And it is so!

In It to Win It

I told you that this journey is compared to being in a race. And anyone who has ever watched track and field in person or in an Olympic game has seen how, for the runner to win when they are close to the finish line, they must reach forward in their upper body. Even though they have not yet physically arrived at the finish line, they strain as they stretch forward to be declared the winner. Are you willing to lean in? People who are eager to lean in and lean forward know that while in the race, they don't have time to cater to their flesh. That is because their energy and strength must be preserved and focused on winning. In this race, we don't have time to cater to our flesh or our own selfish desires.

We must keep the bigger picture before us while on the path. And, while running this race, God wants us to know that this is not a sprint. This race is a marathon. Take your time getting there. It takes time to build a great marriage. Whenever I set out to accomplish something that means a lot to me after everything is said and done, if I believe that I didn't do as well as I liked, my husband has always told me, "Well, Adriene, you'll get better as you go." Somehow, those words were always soothing to me. The reason is that, first of all, they help to remind me that I have yet to reach a state of perfection. It's also because they let me know that if I keep trying to perfect myself while giving my best, I will always have something to reach for and look forward to as I continue to grow in God. If we continue to stay the course, we will get better as we go. That is a promise. Know that in marriage, we never arrive at the finish line when it comes down to building a great marriage. There are no perfect marriages because there are no ideal individuals. Once again, the Apostle Paul said, "No, I am not there yet, but I am willing to press."

I Have Learned

One thing our heavenly Father would have us grasp from the life of the Apostle Paul is that he did not show up on the scene full of faith. Even before coming to know Jesus Christ as his Savior, he had a bold spirit. After Paul (Saul) had the Damascus Road experience, God had to take him through a series of life's challenges that would allow him to go from faith to faith. God specifically told him that he would have to go through many things in life because of His name's sake. So, pressing in the things of God is a learned behavior. If you are a born-again believer, you did not give your life to the Lord and immediately became strong in the Lord and in the power of His might. Nobody can or will ever testify to that. That is why God must allow us to go through some things that do not feel good. Everything that is good for us doesn't always feel good to us. Many things that God says is good for us is not always suitable to us. Am I right about it? But again, God allows us to go through a series of trials and tribulations in this life to build some spiritual muscles. And it is all done by the process of learning because being able to press is definitely a learned behavior.

2 Peter 3:18 says, "But grow in grace, and in the knowledge of our Lord and Savior Jesus Christ...." (GNV) So again, it is about spiritual growth. We grow in grace. We grow in the knowledge of the Lord Jesus Christ. I believe that we grow in God when we take the understanding of the Word of God that we've learned and then apply it to our lives. I have often heard people say, "Knowledge is power!" But, we must realize that the only power that comes from knowledge is the

knowledge we use in our lives that helps us stand in our marriage and in life. I, too, can confess the testimony of the Apostle Paul when he says that he has learned during life's battles. Even while writing, I am yet reaching forward. I am being stretched and have yet to learn, simply because I have yet to arrive. I, too, must press because I have not reached that place of perfect holiness in marriage or life. I have made up my mind to apply continuous effort against all the opposition, against all odds and the forces of darkness coming up against me. I want to win Christ! *1 John 5:4 says, "For everyone born of God is victorious and overcomes the world; and this is the victory that has conquered and overcomes the world — our [continuing, persistent] faith [in Jesus the Son of God]."* (AMP) I speak victory in your life. I declare victory in your relationship and your marriage. I encourage you to *PRESS!*

SHOW ME WHAT YOU'RE MADE OF

In every life, some rain must fall. Nowhere in the Word of God can any of us find a promise where God has promised us that we will live a problem-free life. And that includes *MARRIAGES* as well, my friend!

God will allow us those times in our lives when we are tremendously blessed to have many mountain-top experiences, but our daily lives are lived out with many valley-low experiences. We live in the trenches all while being blessed by God. Therefore, we cannot know what will likely appear next. Most of us could agree that life can be very bittersweet, and life forces us to take the bitter along with the sweet whether we want to or not. Life is not concerned about our feelings, nor is it concerned about our emotions.

I also believe that many of us can agree that God is still a good God regardless of what shows up in our lives! And, no matter what happens, it is always the will of God that we would stay in a perpetual state of praise. It is no wonder why in *Psalms 34:1,* David says, *"I will bless the LORD at all times; His praise shall continually be in my mouth."* (AMP) We were created to praise God. Everything that happens to us during our marriage can help to strengthen our relationship if we have the proper perspective on how we look at each situation. Though every trial can be incredibly challenging and sometimes quite devastating, God will allow us to separate parched lips and muster up praise along the way.

<u>Show and Tell</u>

One day as I was watching television, a commercial came on that I had seen on several different occasions, but I had never really paid much attention to it. But, on this particular day, God began speaking to me as it came on. It was as if the words jumped off the television screen and began ministering to my spirit. I said it before and will repeat it again: when you have an ear to hear, God will speak to you through just about anything or in any situation.

It was a commercial by a food distribution company named Sysco. When I saw this commercial, we were still in the first year of the COVID-19 pandemic. So, in this commercial, Sysco appealed to the viewing audience to support their local restaurants by ordering food from take-out services to keep restaurants open and operating.

As this commercial comes on, they start by saying, "Adversity came to town and said — SHOW ME WHAT YOU'RE MADE OF!" In life and marriage, we must always know adversity will make a grand appearance and show up in our lives from time to time. As I previously stated, trouble, chaos, and misfortune will all show up dressed in the form of adversity. It shows up without any prior warning. It shows up without allowing us to get ourselves more prepared to deal with it or wrap our minds around the situation at hand.

Another thing about adversity is that when it has found our address and decides to pay us a personal visit, we cannot be *exempt* from it. We cannot tell God that we have concluded and therefore have decided that we do not want to *participate* in it, so please allow us to be *excused* from it! We cannot outrun it, and no amount of fasting and prayer will cause us to duck and dodge life's adversities. So, therefore, we must learn through the grace of God and through the power of the Holy Spirit how to find a way to embrace it and overcome it as we stand on the promises of God. When it shows up, it immediately begins to put our faith to the test. Sometimes, it feels as though our faith is backed up against the wall. Other times, it feels as though our faith is on the ropes. There will be times in our marriage when we will find that our faith will seem to be as if we are barely holding on and our marriage is on a life-support system. Have you ever experienced marriage challenges that were so excruciating and difficult to bear that you felt as if your faith was touch and go while the adversity demanded you to show it how much faith you had? It is those times when our walk with God and our quiet times with God will matter the most. Those are the times and the moments when we come to realize that how we have spent those sunny days will determine how well we are able to deal with that stormy day when it's hard to see the light of day. Those are the times when what is *in us* will begin to come *out of us*! Hard times in life and marriage will cause our true colors to start to show while allowing our strengths or weaknesses to be exposed. We can rest assured that adversity will call the real us to be drawn to the front lines of battle. See, sometimes, it is easy to say that we are Christians and to wear our collars and flaunt our titles. It is easy for us to quote the scriptures and speak the Word of God without living by the very words we speak until an actual trial shows up.

At some point in life, what is in us will eventually come out of us in times of adversity. If you think about a sponge, once you put the squeeze on it or it gets to its full capacity, there is no doubt that whatever it is full of will begin to drip out. If it is filled with water, water will start to drip out. If it is filled with Coca-Cola, guess what? Coca-Cola will begin dripping out. And when life squeezes us, it causes our faith to be placed on full display. Therefore, we must stay in a perpetual place of studying God's Word and filling our spirit with the Word of God because we never know when we have to show adversity what we are made of while on the path to greatness.

Your Faith Is Showing

We have all experienced going into a jewelry store looking for an engagement ring, a tennis bracelet, or some other type of jewelry. In all the jewelry stores that I have been in, if the jewelry is costly, you do not have the ability to walk up to the counter and pick it up to take a closer look. Instead, the jewelry is in what you would call "a display case." Therefore, one would walk up to the display case and look at each piece separately to admire its beauty. Likewise, there will be times in our marriage when God will allow our faith to be fully displayed. And like fine jewelry on display for all to see, God often allows our lives to be displayed so that others can see. Some of us are better at keeping things covered, but sometimes, it is much harder to conceal due to the severity of the trial.

It is no secret that God frequently allows the enemy to bring some adversity to help us to get to that next level. I talk about Joseph in another chapter of the book, but just like in Joseph's life, God allowed some adversity to bring him to another level in his faith. As he was having a conversation with his siblings concerning the wrong that they all conspired in to kill him and sell him into slavery, he told them in *Genesis 50:20, "As for you, you meant evil against me, but God meant it for good in order to bring about this present outcome, that many people would be kept alive [as they are this day]."* (AMP) Joseph told them that even though they had one thing in mind for the wrong reasons, God had something else in mind for a better cause and all of the right reasons. I want to encourage you that whatever the enemy shows up within your marriage, whatever plot he has conceived, God allowed it to happen, that His will can come to pass in our lives. God will allow it many times so we can move from being a faith-talker to being a faith-walker. Yet, at other times, He wants to stretch our faith as He calls us further into the deep. In the end, the will of God for our lives will always be for our good and for His glory!

Confident Assurance

If you are reading this book today, I am fully aware that it is written and addressed to help married couples learn how to thrive and survive in their marriages. But, adversity can and does show up in many forms. It can be in the form of a bad diagnosis. It can show up in the form of financial challenges, children going astray, the loss of a loved one, discrimination, hate crimes, etc. God is an all-inclusive God. God wants to touch your life regardless of what you are dealing with or going through. God wants us to have *"Confident Assurance"* in Him. Somebody may ask, "Well, what is a confident assurance?" A confident assurance means no matter what happens, you must know in your heart that God not only can keep your marriage, but He also has the power to do what needs to be done to help you to stand in any area of your life! *Hebrews 11:1 says, "Now faith is the ASSURANCE of things hoped for, the conviction of things not seen."* (ESV) So, when I say we must have a confident assurance, I am speaking about more than just having some wishful thinking about your marriage's health and wholeness. I am talking about getting off the fence of doubt and having an expectation that you can indeed have a blessed marriage. You must know how to encourage yourself in the Lord. You must learn to speak God's word constantly and confidently, regardless of what you see or how you feel. Many marriages have ended in divorce because the couples walk by sight and not by faith. If you are a born-again believer, keep believing God and know through the word of God that you have what it takes on the inside of you to make it by faith. In marriage, we all must have something on the inside of us that knows how to rise to the occasion. We must know how to walk away from and quit keeping company with a "Woe-is-me" attitude and stop feeling sorry for ourselves. Otherwise, the enemy will have a chokehold in our minds, thereby having a chokehold on our marriage, and he will always have the upper hand on us if we do not rise to the occasion. When I say "rise to the occasion," that means learning how to perform well in response to the situation or event that's taking place in your life. Rising to the occasion also means to make the special effort that is required to successfully deal with a difficult situation. Our faith must show up because trials allow us to know what we are working with when it comes down to standing our ground against the adversary.

That is why *Jude 1:20 says, "But you, beloved, build yourselves up on [the foundation of] your most holy faith [continually progress, rise like an edifice higher and higher] pray in the Holy Spirit."* (AMP) If you are a child of God and the Holy Spirit of God lives on the inside of you, can I encourage you today that the same power that raised Christ from the dead also dwells in you? Read that scripture again. It says to *"Build Yourselves Up!"* We have the wherewithal that we do not have to sit around and wait for the pastor to call us. Most times, it's good if they do call. I, myself, on occasion have found it necessary to call others to help to build me up in the spirit. The Bible tells us that two are better than one. But, we do not have to keep bugging our best friend; we don't have to keep ringing someone else's phone off the hook when God has given us the authority to build ourselves up! That's powerful! God has given you us what it takes to build ourselves up on our most holy faith by praying in the Holy Ghost.

Whose Fight Is It Anyway

I remember one time when I knew this young lady and quickly became fond of her. She was a beautiful lady inside and out. I had been saved at that time for about twenty years. When I asked her if she was saved and if she knew the Lord in the pardon of her sins, she said she was saved. I could remember how she was having some severe challenges in her life. She was particularly challenged in her marriage. Her husband did not think twice about disrespecting her in front of others. She was mentally, verbally, and emotionally abused. So, I tried to be a spiritual mentor to her. I wanted to avail myself to her by ministering to her regularly and praying for her through all of the adversity she had to endure. Quite honestly, I don't know how she did not crack up. So, one day, she called me, crying profusely. I could not understand a word she was saying through her crying and the grief she was expressing. All I knew was that she was being abused again. So, because I could not understand her, I immediately went into prayer mode. I started praying and asking God to touch her and strengthen her. I asked God to heal her, comfort her, and direct her path. I was doing some serious spiritual warfare on her behalf. Then I began praying in tongues just in case I missed something I should have been petitioning God about on her behalf.

I stood in the gap, prayed, and encouraged her for a prolonged period of time throughout the years because God does call us to bear one another's burden. After I did not see any change in her situation and when I saw that she didn't try to go to church, seek professional counseling, or try to better her situation by putting her faith into action, I became spiritually drained. So, one day, when she called, after I finished praying for her, God allowed me to see a vision concerning her situation and what role I was playing in her life. And right before me, He showed me a picture of me in fighting in a boxing ring. While I was in the boxing ring fighting, she was standing on the *outside of the ropes,* watching me while *I was fighting her battle!* And it was at that point that God told me to totally release her to Him. My point here is praying friends, prayer warriors, and pastors are lovely to have in your life, but God has given us the ability to build ourselves up on our most holy faith. And what they add to our lives to help strengthen us should be lagniappe to what we are already doing by faith. If we believe it, we are strong in the Lord when we are operating in *"His Might"* as opposed to our power. I like what Joyce Meyer says when she says, "You can either be *pitiful,* or you can be *powerful,* but you can't be both!" God leaves it to us to make a choice.

Today, I want you to know and realize *who you are* and *whose you are*. Right now, I challenge you to open your mouth and declare and decree, "God did not bring me this far to leave me! God said that He would never leave me nor forsake me. I can cast all my cares upon Him because I know that He loves me. And I believe that what He has done for others, even in the midst of adversity, He will also do the same for me!"

God is Alpha and Omega. He is the beginning and the end. He has already declared our end from our beginning, and all He requires of us is to walk it out by faith! This fight is a done deal. This Christian battle is a fixed fight. And what I love about the Lord is that nothing can ever catch Him off guard. Nothing can ever take Him by surprise. No one can ever give Him any advice He does not already know. Isn't it good to know that God never sleeps nor slumbers? So, can you tell me what do you believe is *too hard* for your God? Trouble did not come to stay, but it came to pass, and *"This Too Shall Pass!"*

Ephesians 3:20 tells us, *"Now unto Him that is able to do exceeding abundantly above all that we ask or think, according to the power that worketh in us."* (KJV) Working the Word of God in your life must be a continuous process, and putting the Word into practice only a few times concerning your situation isn't good enough. In other words, it is not a one-and-done type of situation. If you desire to keep getting results, you must continue to work the Word that the Word will continue to work on your behalf.

I want to call your attention to the scripture that says, *"God is able."* That was a perfect place to shout, "Hallelujah!" The scripture does not stop there. It goes on to say that God is able to do exceedingly abundantly above all that we ask or think, according to the power that *worketh* in us. I am saying that God is promising us that there is no question of His power and ability to do what He said He would do. He is letting us know that we can't dig deep enough in our thought life or our asking ability to formulate the words or to think higher above His ability to answer our prayer and bring about the things we have asked for, thought about, or sought Him about during worship. Whoa! I know that was a lot there! Because His thoughts are higher than our thoughts and His ways are higher than ours, we do not have the wherewithal to think or ask God for anything that He cannot far outweigh or supersede in His ability to deliver.

I believe that many of us do not go to the latter part of the scripture to understand what is required of us for God to deliver. The scripture says that He is able to do it exceedingly abundantly above *"according to"* what is *working* or what is continuing to work on the inside of us. It's as if God is saying to us, "Show Me What You're Working With!" His keeping His end of the deal is *"based upon"* or *"contingent upon"* what we have working on the inside of us by faith! My God, I pray somebody has an ear to hear this. So, what's working on the inside of you when it comes down to what you believe God to do in and for your marriage? Is fear working in you? Are doubt and unbelief constantly working in you? Is a bad attitude or being unforgiving working inside of you when it comes to your mate when dealing with adversity? God wants us to show Him how much faith we work with amid adversity. I am still speaking about showing adversity what we're made of and how we can allow our faith level to rise to the occasion!

On the other side of this, is faith continuing to work inside of you? Do you have an expectation working on the inside of you? Do you believe that there will be a PERFORMANCE of His Word and that He is still in the miracle-working business? *Mark 9:23 says, "If thou canst believe, all things are possible to [them] that believeth."* (KJV) All things are possible to the man or the woman of God who CONTINUES TO BELIEVE! I have a spiritual mentor who always says that "All believers don't believe." God will do His part based upon and contingent upon what you and I have working and continuing to work on the inside of us.

Faith in Action

When it comes down to Christianity, it is all based on faith. It starts with faith, and it ends with faith. The Bible tells us that without faith, it is impossible to please God. Many times, in marriage, faith is the missing ingredient. More often than not, it is the missing link. Faith must be present to see the hand of God move in your marriage. That's a short statement with a lot of punch. We have heard certain scriptures concerning faith so many times that some folks have become desensitized. Some of us have become so desensitized that the very teaching about faith goes over our heads. We began thinking and saying to ourselves, "Oh, I heard that before." We cannot become too familiar with the Word of God because if we do, the Word will not have any effect in our lives. *Hebrews 11:1 says, "Now faith is the assurance (title deed, confirmation) of things hoped for (divinely guaranteed) and the evidence of things not seen [the conviction of their reality — faith comprehends as fact what cannot be experienced by the physical* senses]." (AMP) *Hebrew 11:6 says, "But without faith, it is impossible to [walk with God and] please Him, for whoever comes [near] to God must [necessarily] believe that God exists and that He rewards those who [earnestly and diligently] seek Him."* (AMP) I encourage you to study these scriptures and allow your faith to come alive.

From Pain to Pursuit

A pastor once said something in his book that totally blessed my life. In his book, he stated, "God does not respond to our pain, but He responds to our pursuit." That may be hard for some people to wrap their heads around. That is not to say that God is not concerned or deeply touched by the things we go through. The Bible tells us that God is love. So, God does care. In all my years of being saved, I would always hear people say, "God may not come when you want Him to come, but He's always on time." God could have very well shown up for many people right when they wanted Him to and when they needed him the most. But, for many people, God does not do a hundred-yard dash when we are in pain. He is not always "Johnny on the spot." If you believe that He constantly shows up on time, ask Mary and Martha. In John 11, the Bible tells us that when Lazarus was sick, Mary and Martha sent word to Jesus to come to see about Lazarus. While I am not one hundred percent sure, Lazarus had to be suffering some pain and agony for the sisters to call for Jesus. But yet, Lazarus died. I believe it's important for me to say that God's love for us has nothing to do with when He's going to show up on our behalf. Some of you need to read that last statement again! *John 11: 5 says, "Now Jesus loved and was concerned about Martha and her sister and Lazarus [and considered them dear friends.]"* (AMP) He loved them and was concerned about them, yet He stayed two extra days. He loved them, yet He allowed Lazarus to die. Again, never think that God does not love you simply because He's not showing up for you when and how you believe He should show up.

My point here is that as we trust God in our marriages, God is looking for us to put our faith into action. We must know how to put some feet to our faith. Faith is the word of God that we believe, but there must also be some corresponding action that goes along with our beliefs. Amid the pain and the heartache, we have to know how to pursue after God. To follow God, we must learn how to chase after God. It can also mean to search for, to seek after, or to stalk. God loves us so much that He chases after us and longs for us. Can I tell you that He also wants us to reciprocate that love through the chase? It reminds me of the song by Teddy Pendergrass ("When Somebody Loves You Back") that says, "It's so good lovin' somebody when somebody loves you back." I believe that when we get desperate enough to see the hand of God move in our marriages, we will take on stalking-like characteristics in our pursuit of God.

God is concerned about the pain that we experience. But, pain does not move God as much as the faith we display during the chasing process does because the chasing process involves faith to be on the scene. There must be some spiritual activity that is taking place on our behalf. So, right there in the midst of the tears, right there in the midst of the strife and the misunderstanding in your marriage, you'd better know how to have some spiritual activity that is taking place to help you to be able to stand. Faith moves the hand of God when we believe that our tears, depression, and heaviness are adequate enough to get God's attention. I told you that life would require you to show what you are made of and prove whether you can stand. Therefore, faith must be out there, front and center. Even through the tears, learn how to cause your faith to lock in.

We cannot expect God to come and show up and show out when faith is not in operation. *James 2:14–18 says, "What is the benefit, my fellow believers, if someone claims to have faith but has no [good] works [as evidence]? Can that [kind of] faith save him? [No, a mere claim of faith is not sufficient — genuine faith produces good works.] (15)If a brother or sister is without [adequate] clothing and lacks [enough] food for each day, (16) And one of you says to them, 'Go in* peace [with my blessing], keep warm and feed yourselves,' but he does not give them the necessities for the body, what good does that do? (17) So too, faith, if it does not have works [to back it up], is by itself dead [inoperative and ineffective]. (18) But someone may say, "You [claim to] have faith, and I have [good] works; show me your [alleged] faith without the works [if you can], and I will show you my faith by my works [that is, by what I do]." (AMP) WOW!

God is looking for some "good works" to back up what we believe Him for because faith without works is dead. If there aren't any works to accompany our faith, that means that we have resulted in becoming a hearer of the word and not a doer. We must do something about that which we have heard. Can you open your mouth and say, "I'm in pursuit of God?"

Come Forth

Just for a moment, I would like to revisit the story concerning Mary, Martha, and Lazarus when it comes down to going from pain to pursuit. In John, chapter 11, the Bible tells us that after

Jesus finally got back to Bethany, the place where Lazarus died, He was finally ready to raise Lazarus from the dead. In *John 11:39,* Jesus gave Mary and Martha something to do so He could see their faith! He told them to *"Take away the stone."* And after they took some action, the Bible says that Jesus lifted up his eyes and began to pray to the Father after they decided to participate in the miracle. If you read *John 11:43,* it says, Jesus shouted with a loud voice, *"Lazarus, come out!"* Notice what Jesus did not do. He did not go into the grave to carry Lazarus out. He didn't go in seeking and searching to see if Lazarus heard him or if Lazarus was indeed going to come out. Even being dead, Lazarus had to listen to the voice of Jesus and come out of that dead situation. You may have a deadly problem going on in your marriage, but if you can hear the voice of Jesus, just like Lazarus, you can come out! You may be in pain and your situation may have died, but God is not necessarily obligated to come in and carry you to a place of safety if you are void of faith. And just like Lazarus, your marriage may be in a place to where it's stinking by now, but by faith, we must hear the voice of God and come out of those dead situations in our marriage that seek to keep us bound. One thing that I can certainly appreciate about the story concerning Lazarus is that Lazarus was moving forward toward Jesus even while he was still bound in the grave cloths. He was moving toward Jesus even being a stinky mess, but he had to start taking steps of faith before Jesus said "Loose him, and let him go." My God! We often want to be loosed from our circumstances without taking any steps of faith toward the One who is able to deliver us and set us free. Notice here that Jesus was not speaking to Lazarus, but He was commanding the clothing of death to loose Lazarus and let him go. If we desire to come away from the stinky mess that the trials of marriage can bring on, we must be willing to start taking steps toward Jesus, even if you still have on the grave cloths. What am I saying here? I'm saying taking steps toward Jesus will always precede being delivered from what seeks to keep us bound. Do it by faith because God wants us to show Him what we're made of by hearing and obeying His voice. Just like Lazarus, when we decide to get up from that dead place in our marriage and start taking steps toward Jesus, he will speak to those dead situations and say "Loose them, and let them go!"

I Have No One to Help

In the book of John, chapter 5, you will read about when Jesus was in Jerusalem, there was a pool called "Bethesda." And at the Pool of Bethesda, the Bible says there were many sick people there who were in need of healing. Some people were blind, others were impotent, and others had withered body parts. And when the angel would come down to stir the water, whoever was the first person to get into the water was made free of whatever disease or infirmity that was plaguing them. So, in *John 5:5–9*, Jesus begins conversing with a man. It says in verse (5), *"There was a certain man there who had been ill for 38 years. (6) When Jesus noticed him lying there [helpless], knowing that he had been in that condition for a long time, He said to him, 'Do you want to get well?' (7) The invalid answered, 'Sir, I have no one to put me in the pool when the water is stirred up, and while I am coming [to get into it myself], someone else steps down ahead of me." (8) Jesus said to him, 'Get up; pick up your pallet and walk.' (9) "Immediately the man was healed and recovered his strength, and picked up his pallet and walked."* (AMP)

So again, Jesus told him, *"Pick up your bed and walk."* In other words, I want you to act and do something that will cause you to take part in your own deliverance. Even though the man was trying to do something on his own, apparently, something wasn't working in his favor. It was as if Jesus was saying to the man, "You take the very words that I am speaking to you, put them into action, and then you can look for some results." If you do not put your faith into action by following God's directions, you cannot expect any results. When you read the story about the Pool of Bethesda, it would seem as if when Jesus saw all of these people who were ill, He would have shown up on the scene and healed all of them because He loved them. Jesus was still looking for them to get their faith involved in the healing process, which was the reason they had to make their way into the pool. When we accept the Word of God, we will begin to take some action on what we say we believe. And when we start to take some action, we will begin to see the hand of God move.

Changing What I Cannot Accept

The Bible tells us in Mark chapter 2 that when Jesus returned to Capernaum, the news of his being in town began to be noised abroad. And the place where Jesus went to minister, the Bible says that there were so many people there that you could not even get in. *Mark 2:3 says, "Then they came, bringing to Him a paralyzed man, who was being carried by four men. (4) When they were unable to get to Him because of the crowd, they removed the roof above Jesus; and when they had dug out an opening, they let down the mat on which the paralyzed man was lying. (5) When Jesus saw their [active] faith [springing from confidence in Him], He said to the paralyzed man, 'Son, your sins are forgiven.'"* (AMP) Verse 5 says that *Jesus saw their active faith.* When Jesus saw how they began searching for and seeking another way, their actions got His attention. If I could say this differently, their positive spiritual activity caught His attention.

One day, I was in an online business seminar, and I heard somebody say something that would forever change the trajectory of my life. The guy said, "Many of us have learned how to accept those things that we cannot change instead of changing those things that we cannot accept." The story about the four men who let the paralyzed man down through the roof perfectly illustrates what the gentleman said in the online seminar. There were some people who showed up where Jesus was teaching the Word of God; they turned around and went back home when they saw that they could not get in to see Jesus. They stopped short of receiving a blessing. These people went back home because they had the mindset that they were willing to accept what they believed they could not change. While they were disappointed when they saw so many people congregated at the front door; these other four guys were already in the process of seeing how they could switch gears. All of the people who turned around and went back home started thinking and saying to themselves "We can't." I'm sure they started wondering what would have happened if they would have gotten there an hour earlier, maybe they would have had an opportunity to see Jesus. The other men who were not willing to quit and give up, instead of them saying, "We can't," started thinking to themselves, "How can we?" Their pursuit, desperation, and active faith caused them to devise a plan to change the things they could not accept. And guess what? What blesses me in this story is the fact that the paralyzed man was not Jesus' primary focus. The four men's active faith showed Jesus what they were made of, and their faith in action was the thing that got the attention of Jesus. Their trust in Jesus caused Him to respond accordingly. Jesus always responds to faith.

When there is trouble in paradise, it is not that God does not care about what you're going through. It's just that God is more interested in your "Pursuit" than He is in your nursing the pain without any positive spiritual activity or any corresponding action. In *John 11:39,* when Jesus told Martha, *"'Take away the stone,'"* her response to Him was, *'Lord, by this time there will be an offensive odor, for he has been dead four days!'[It is hopeless.]"* John 11:40 says, *"Jesus said to her, 'Did I not say to you that if you believe [in Me], you will see the glory of God [the expression of His excellence]?'"* That's my prayer for you. You don't have to accept the feeling of helplessness and hopelessness in your marriage. Don't allow the stench of your trial nor the amount of time you have been dealing with your situation sway you to believe it's a hopeless situation. Jesus said to Martha, "If you believe in Me, you will see the glory of God." Begin chasing after God because "faith" is an action word. When adversity shows up and asks you to show it what you're made of, active faith and your pursuit after God will have an opportunity to rise to the occasion. Again, the Word of God says, *"Show me your works without your faith, and I will show you my works by my faith."* Have faith in God. You can do this!

I am led to pray as I close this particular chapter. Dear God, I pray for every married couple, every single or engaged individual who read the pages of this book. I pray that You perform a miracle in their lives and, if necessary, in their marriage. I pray that when adversity shows up, You will arise and allow every one of their enemies to be scattered. I pray that no man would put asunder or separate what You have joined together! God, my prayer is that when adversity shows up, by the power of the Holy Spirit, You will help them to walk by faith and not by sight. Help them to stand still and see the salvation of the Lord in Jesus' Name! Father, allow them to take on the mindset that they will no longer accept what they cannot change, but they will begin to pray, looking and searching out ways to change those things in their lives and in their marriage that they cannot accept. Help them to know that only when they are strong in YOU and the power of YOUR MIGHT can they show adversity what they are really made of by having the God-kind of faith!

HARD WORK

There is an old Gatorade commercial that I simply love. It ministers volumes to me. The commercial features Dwayne Wade, Serena Williams, Derek Jeter, and a few more athletes. In this commercial, you see the scoreboard lighting up with the two words saying "WINNING IS." Then, you will hear an alarm clock going off at 5:30 a.m. The athletes wake up early in the morning at daybreak to put in the hard work and all of the untiring efforts in the very thing that causes them to be the best and in that which makes them the greatest. They hop out of bed and begin their exercise regimen by running, lifting weights, and playing tennis. They are shown doing push-ups and sit-ups, jumping rope, and doing everything it takes to cause them to excel in their various careers and the game of sports, all while drinking their Gatorade. It shows us precisely what it takes to separate ordinary people from those who are the greatest. I don't know about you, but I don't believe that God

called us to be average. God called us to
greatness!

In this Gatorade commercial, after you read
the sign saying, "Winning Is," you will hear them
singing and repeating the words "Work, work."
Again, what they are trying to convey to us is that
"WINNING IS HARD WORK." And if you want to
win in marriage and life, you must be willing to
put in the strenuous efforts that cause one to win.
You must be willing to put in the hard work when
you don't feel like it. You must be ready to push
past your limitations and find the strength to go
further than you ever thought possible. Winners
are willing to wake up early, when others are still
asleep. They are eager to lose in certain areas of
life that they may win where it matters the most.
They are willing to sacrifice where, when, and
what others are not willing to sacrifice. They have
made up their minds that they're not satisfied
with walking away with a participation ribbon to
show that they have participated or competed,
but they want to win. I submit to you that there
is a price to be paid for being able to run the

fastest, jump the highest, and be the best. Therefore, this commercial is so befitting to start this chapter of "HARD WORK," simply because winning is hard work. Winning at marriage will also require the same hard work and diligence to be triumphant. I can assure you that those who are winning at marriage and those who have healthy marriages are the ones who are willing to work the hardest to walk in victory. In the sports arena, the ones who win are the ones who are willing to take a licking and keep on ticking because they see beyond the here and now. They know how to ignore certain things. They continue to show up and continue playing the game even when their bodies are racked with pain. They have been trained in what to do so that they can win. Their entire lives are built around their purpose and what they're trying to accomplish.

Please make no mistake about it; marriage is hard work. It does not matter what it looks like on the outside to others. It does not matter what your married family members, friends, or loved ones have told you. Marriage is not a cakewalk.

Yes, it yields some excellent fruit if you are willing to put in the effort continuously. But it is not for the faint at heart. And it is definitely not a one-and-done type situation where you work hard at it for a specific amount of time, and you have arrived for the duration.

Today, many couples are writing their own wedding vows. Have you ever pondered on the fact that many married couples have taken vows that say, "Marriage should not be entered into unadvisedly or lightly, but honestly and reverently?" Many of us have promised to be here for better or for worse. And, for those who have spoken those vows, have you ever wondered why you said that in your wedding vows? One reason it should not be entered into unadvisedly or lightly, but honestly and reverently, is because marriage is serious business! I love being married to my husband. We get along quite well most of the time. We genuinely believe that we were made for each other. We have more good days together as a couple than trying days. Even when the trials of marriage bring me to tears and always to my knees, I refuse to call them bad days because we are winning or we are learning, but we're never losing! I can admit that it's quite challenging to keep that perspective when we are smack-dab in the midst of a trial due to emotions that are raging. Too many couples see trying days as a sad thing as opposed to what I call "Teachable moments!" Even when I have tears in my eyes and I am unsure of what's going on, I still see every trail as a teachable moment that God will use, if I am willing to learn and grow. We should always be in a perpetual place of learning from the last trial in order that it will help us endure in the next test that is sure to come. When we love God, it is all working together for our good despite the pain and the severity of what's taking place.

I can testify to you that there will be many days that you are going to have to endure those trying days before better even shows up and make its presence known. In every marriage, if your goals and your desires are to win, you must not only be willing to give of yourself, but you must be willing to give yourself away. ALL OF YOU! I always used to hear people say that marriage should be 50/50. And to that statement, I am sensing the need to really park right here for a spell, so please bear with me. I cannot help but wonder who came up with that silly notion! I'm really not trying to be funny here. I believe someone was sitting around one day and began thinking that because fifty plus fifty equals one hundred, they felt that was sufficient for a marriage to be whole and complete, but not so! I do not know about you, but I denounced that notion and way of thinking long ago. I discovered not long after saying "I do," that if we're both ALL IN, it makes for a better marriage union.

If I had limited myself to giving just fifty percent and my husband is giving fifty percent, well, contrary to this widely held belief, that marriage is in big trouble! That does not sound like a commitment at all. Fifty percent is far from giving my absolute best to God and my mate. Giving fifty percent of me to my spouse means that I have stopped short of the expectations of God when it comes down to having a blessed marriage. I must be willing to give more of myself to become the best version of myself. Fifty percent is not enough to keep the enemy at bay. And it's not enough to cause the enemy even to begin thinking about wanting to flee! You better hear me!

The Bible tells us in *James 4:7*, *"So submit to [the authority of] God. Resist the devil [stand firm against him] and he will flee from you."* (AMP) I know I am pressing the issue here, but I mean to do so because I have heard too many people talk about how marriage is 50/50. It's sad to say, but many of those same people I have heard say, "Marriage is 50/50," marriages that are falling apart because fifty percent just won't do. The Bible tells us that we perish because of a lack of knowledge. I am still going. So, would you say that giving fifty percent of yourself in marriage is considered submitting yourselves to God wholeheartedly? Would you say giving less than ALL OF YOU is considered to be doing an excellent job of resisting the enemy? The Bible tells us in *1 Peter 5:8, "Your adversary the devil, as a roaring lion, walketh about, seeking whom he may devour....*" (KJV) So, giving fifty percent is an open door for the enemy to step in and wreak havoc in your marriage. I wholeheartedly believe these days and times that we're living in, one of us or both of us must be willing to go well beyond giving one hundred percent of ourselves because the enemy is so cunning. We must genuinely learn how to flip the script and beat the adversary at his own game. I am reminded of the Motel 6 commercial where Tom Bodett says, "We'll leave the light on for you." Don't give the enemy the green light or an open door to drop in by simply giving fifty percent because that is a recipe for disaster! I pray that someone was set free from the 50/50 myth! A blessed marriage will require all of you and then some!

Pure Inspiration

At the very beginning of my writing journey many years ago, I was genuinely inspired by a much older lady at the gym. I cannot remember her name, so I will call her Ms. Mary. Many years ago, I always had the desire to get back into the gym to work out. I talked about it for years without putting any actions behind my words until my husband, Shawn, purchased us a gym membership. When I first started going back to the gym, as you can imagine, it wasn't easy. Starting a new gym regimen is all about first getting your mind right before any results can be seen, expected, or experienced. It also consists of putting in the time, ensuring that you are disciplined enough, getting past being sore after strenuous workouts, and even changing your diet. The theme at the gym at that time was "Getting Results and Loving It!" Well, I had my mind made up that I would get the results I so desperately desired. So, I began with step classes. I especially enjoyed the step classes. It was a good workout regimen for helping with the cardiovascular system and getting the heart pumping, all while dancing and moving to some amazing music. Then, I moved on to taking spin classes and body-pumps classes. The spin class is all about indoor cycling and the body-pump class is designed to work out every part of your body while using weights, doing squats, sit-ups, push-ups, lunges, etc. When I started the body-pump class, I tell you, I had to encounter a whole new type of beast. The body-pump class is where I first met Ms. Mary. If I had to guess her age, she appeared to be in the neighborhood of seventy years old. She was a noticeably short lady who always looked a bit frail to me. But, when it came down to lifting those weights and keeping up with the instructor, without fail, Ms. Mary would always put me to shame. I found myself struggling to keep up. After lifting so many weights, my arms would feel as light as a piece of spaghetti. My arms, legs, and every muscle in my body would always be left feeling very tired and weak after the body-pump class. As we would transition ever so swiftly from rounds of lifting weights to doing push-ups, back into squats and push-ups again, I would find myself getting very dizzy and light-headed. And when I would glance over at Ms. Mary, all I could say was, "She was on it!" She did not appear to be breathing heavily at all as I was breathing. I often thought to myself, "Girl, you don't know what you've gotten yourself into here." I cannot tell you how many times in every class that I repeatedly looked at the exit door. So often, I thought about politely picking up my exercise equipment, putting everything back in its proper place, and just suffering from the sheer embarrassment of defeat. I wanted nothing more than to head out of the door to call it quits in every class. If I could be honest with you, the only thing that made me persevere at that point was not the results I was looking for, but it was Ms. Mary. I kept saying to myself, "If Ms. Mary can do it and if she has the capability of hanging tough, surely I can do it too." You can call it competition if you'd like to, but I called it pure inspiration!

At that time, I was about forty years old. Ms. Mary was my motivation to keep on going. She lived right in the next block. One day, as I was passing her home, I watched how she was taken away from her home and placed into an ambulance. I would often see her being taken away in an ambulance. Unfortunately, that was the last time, because sadly to say, she passed away. But not before I had the opportunity to tell her how her tenacity encouraged me in ways she could not have imagined. I am so grateful that I had the chance to share with her how she inspired me to start writing a book about how to persevere in marriage by simply watching how she persevered at the gym. You see, the concept is the same. The mindset and the tenacity are the same. You need the same discipline in life, whether it is at the gym or in marriage, if you plan on winning and being victorious.

Those first three times I did the body-pump class, I remember getting home only to get myself something else to drink, and I would literally plop down on the sofa while my head was spinning. At that time, I tell you that I felt so discouraged and so defeated. Therefore, I found myself doing plenty of negative self-talk. I found myself saying, "Under no circumstances will I be attending that body-pump class again!" I also kept wishing and praying that my good friend Tammy would not call my phone to ask me to go, either. And every time my phone would ring the morning of the class, I could remember how my nerves would be rattled because I knew the voice on the other end would be saying, "Are you going today?" Even though my nerves were rattled, I do believe accountability is critical in life when you are looking to get some positive results that you can love. I thank God for her because we all need people around us who are willing to hold us accountable while pushing us into greatness. I often fall short when it comes down to being disciplined with going to the gym, but she was and still is a good accountability coach.

One day after a challenging class, I was exhausted as I lay on my sofa with every muscle in my body racked with pain. As I lay on the sofa, I can say that was the day the Lord started birthing this book into my spirit concerning marriage. He began relating so many of my gym experiences to the experiences that I was having in my marriage at that time. The truth of the matter was there were many times in my marriage I would think about calling it quits. There were many times that I felt so discouraged and defeated. And yes, I cried out in agony and pain while thinking to myself that this was much too hard for me to bear and endure. I have had times and moments in my marriage when I can say that my very soul actually ached with pain. And because of the severity of the trials and the tribulations, the enemy would tell me to take my belongings and head for the door. I must say that I am not and never was one to blurt out the word "divorce" in anger or otherwise, but nevertheless, it was tough for me to stay and to stand. God would do just as He does today. He speaks to me through many everyday life events. God is always speaking, but are we listening?

During one of those painful moments, I could remember going outside one day in my backyard, where my husband was planting tomatoes, green onions, strawberries, peaches, and bell peppers, just to name a few. And as I walked over to the bell peppers against the fence with tears in my eyes, the Lord began speaking to me. The bell peppers still needed to be fully grown. At that time, they were very tiny. I'm talking about amazingly small. As I stared at the bell peppers, the Lord spoke to me and said, "This bell pepper is in the beginning stages of growth. It is not fully developed yet. Can you get excited about what it is *going to become?*" He continued by asking me, "Can you see the end results and be excited about that right now?" I said, "Yes, Lord!" The bell pepper experience within itself was one of the defining moments that caused me to stand. Whoever would have thought that a bell pepper would strengthen your faith and help you to stand strong while you're waiting on God? God is so amazing! But again, the bell pepper experience alone encouraged me by letting me know that, by faith, if I was willing to patiently wait for my change to come, things would get better in my marriage. I tried to believe in God for the better with everything within me. The bell pepper experience let me know that we must see it in the realm of the Spirit before manifestation would occur in the natural. And, if I could get excited about that bell pepper's growth process, I could get excited about what God was yet doing in my marriage in its infant stages.

I can remember those times of frustration that we endured. The pain would sometimes cause me to plop down in the bed with my head spinning. And just as I would experience at the gym, I would wonder if I wanted to keep returning to it again to get the desired results I so fervently prayed about repeatedly. I really wanted to get some results that I could fall in love with, but I knew I had to keep it moving while remaining persistent. I knew if I was going to get those results that I saw far off, I could not quit. More importantly, I knew I could not continue with the thought process of heading for the door whenever things became too complicated and challenging for me to bear. How persuaded are you that God will help you with plan A if you stop thinking about and meditating on plan B? I have discovered early on that if you always have a plan B, an off-ramp, or an exit strategy top of mind, those same strategies you keep meditating on would arise first in your thoughts before God's word, God's power, and God's ability would arise. The enemy will do his best to persuade you to implement those strategies every time an argument occurs if you don't practice keeping the Word of God at the forefront of your mind. We must be able to lock into God's promises regardless of how it feels. We must be cautious about what we're keeping our minds on and what we decide to magnify. We cannot keep considering other options when God has not given us those options to take just because we are tired, hurt, wounded, or angry. Those are not reasons God has given believers to get out of a covenant marriage relationship. I told you that marriage is demanding work. Again, it yields stunning and impressive results when you're willing to work continuously.

Another defining and life-changing moment that the Lord shared with me about Ms. Mary is that she did not start out being able to lift those heavy weights. In other words, she didn't start in beast mode. She had to start slowly as she gradually worked her way to the place where she was, which again was beast mode in my estimation. Even though that should be obvious to us all, that was still life-changing for me because it gave me hope that the "little" really does matter. God tells us in His Word that we should not despise the day of small beginnings. A small beginning is still a beginning, and that's what matters the most.

I encourage those of you who are thinking about heading for the door and calling it quits to stay and stand because great marriages are not born, but they are made. They are made one day at a time. Standing ability should be developed one argument at a time when we learn from it. Great marriages are made from one season of life to the next season of life. You might not know it, but with every heartbreak that you endure, if you follow the promptings of God, that heartbreak will make your marriage more potent than it was before your heart ever began to suffer. I know it doesn't feel like it, but God allows us to become stronger and stronger as we continue to stand. He will begin to give you new strategies as He undergirds you as you continue to stand. But, you must be willing to put in the demanding work. You must be willing to discipline yourself with prayer and seek the face of God. You must be ready to transform your mindset and avoid negative self-talk. You must be willing and obedient to do what it takes according to God's Word. How desperate is your desire for your marriage to be transformed into "beast mode" in the realm of the Spirit, just as Ms. Mary was from putting in the demanding work at the gym because winning is hard work!

Facing the Giants

One of my greatest movies of all time is "Facing the Giants." I mean, I absolutely love this movie! I can watch it repeatedly because I always pick up another nugget that blesses me every time I watch it.

"Facing the Giants" is a movie about a football team having a terrible season. One of the things that blessed me about this dynamic picture is when this football team found themselves in a make-or-break situation that would cause the entire football season to be on the line. They were at a fork in the road where they had to go left or go right. They had to choose whether they wanted to win or whether they were willing to continue accepting a loss. They had to decide if they were willing to put some feet to their faith to get the good results that the team so desperately desired or if they were going to continue operating with a "woe-is-me" attitude.

One of the things that I personally took away from watching this picture is how God Himself shows us how to handle the giants in life. He shows us how to operate in faith when we are facing an opponent who seems to be overwhelming to us or a trial that appears to be more than we believe we are able or capable of handling. It is no secret that in life and marriage, we all will come to a place where we will have to face some giants. No one is exempt. Facing giants in life are inevitable. "Facing the Giants" shows us how to go through what we go through. Too many times, we face the giants with our heads hung down. Many of us have grown accustomed to looking down, acting down, and talking down. But we do not have to go that route. We can choose to go through, like a mighty woman of God

I know, who always says, "We can Believe God or Believe God!" I want to go through my trials believing in God. How many of you know that there is no better way to face the giants in your marriages than to believe in God for the outcome after we have done all?

The team featured in this movie was amid a losing season. And because this football team was experiencing a losing season, the players began to talk down and act down. The defeat that was taking place inside of them began manifested itself on the football team, the practice field, the games, and throughout the team from player to player. It goes without saying that they did not know who they were individually or as a team. The coach, who believed in Christ, slowly introduced the team to the Lord. They began implementing prayer and studying the Word of God. Yet, they greatly struggled to walk with that winning attitude. As the coach kept ministering God's Word to the team and building them up, a miraculous change began taking place.

The Death Crawl

In one movie scene, the team was going through the motions. They lost so many games that they stopped believing in themselves individually and in the team as a whole. They were at the place in the season where they were about to play a school named Wesley. This game would determine who would win the entire season. Many of them were all but sure that they were about to be defeated again! So, as they sat on the ground conversing with a lot of negative self-talk again, one player asked the team leader, "So Brock, how strong is Wesley?" Brock says, "They're a lot stronger than we are!" So, the coach of the team, who overheard this conversation, asked Brock if he had already written off the season. Brock responded, "Not if I knew that we could beat them." The coach then called Brock and Jeremy to do what they call "The Death Crawl." The death crawl was when one person would get on the football field, starting at the one-yard line, and start crawling up the football field to a specified place on their hands and feet with another player on their back. Their knees were not allowed to touch the ground at all. They would usually crawl to the thirty or the fifty-yard line. From what I gathered, the coach made them do the death crawl to show the team they had the capability to win. It was to show them that they could do anything they wanted to do if they only believed in themselves by putting their minds into accomplishing what seemed to be impossible. The coach was trying to get them to believe again.

As Brock and Jeremy began preparing themselves to do the death crawl, Brock told the coach that he could go to the fifty-yard line without Jeremy on his back. The coach said, "I think you can go to the fifty-yard line *with* Jeremy on your back." Not only did the coach want Brock to crawl to the fifty-yard line with Jeremy strapped to his back, but he also wanted him to do it while being blindfolded as well. The only requirement the coach had for Brock was that he would give it all he had and would not quit until he had absolutely nothing left in him. The coach wanted him to keep going even if he believed that he had already made it to the fifty-yard line. Brock asked the coach why he wanted him to go past the fifty-yard line when the fifty-yard line was required of him. The coach told him it was because he did not want him to give up at the fifty-yard line if he had it in him to go farther. My Lord, I pray somebody is catching this revelation.

The coach says, "Brock, do your best. Give me your very best." So, Brock, with Jeremy strapped on his back, started the death crawl up the field. When he got so far and began feeling a little pain, he hollered, "Am I almost there, coach?" The coach says, "Don't you worry about that. You just keep on moving!" As Brock was crawling, his muscles began to burn even more! The weight of Jeremy strapped on his back began to become more than he could handle. He told the coach he could not make it because it hurt too badly. The coach kept encouraging him by beating on the turf, saying, "Don't you give up on me Brock. You can do this! You keep on moving! You keep going!" Brock said, "Coach, I'm running out of strength!" When Brock screamed that he was running out of strength, the coach responded to that statement, "Well, you negotiate with your body, and you find some more strength. You keep on moving!" WOW! The coach was down on his hands and knees the whole time, keeping up with Brock, screaming at him not to quit. He was screaming at him to keep going and encouraging him not to give up or give in. And finally, when Brock had given it his all, when he fell to the ground in exhaustion and agony, he lay on the ground, crying to his coach vehemently. With tears streaming from his eyes as he was apologizing to his coach that he couldn't go any farther, the coach said, "Look up, Brock, you're in the end-zone!" My God! I'm sensing chills running up my arms. What an amazing story of encouragement! Brock crawled all the way to the finish line when he didn't think he could! Hallelujah! The coach told him, "Brock, don't you ever tell me what you cannot do." He said, "You're the leader of this team. And if you start talking down and speaking doubt, so will they." I declare and decree to you right now, the one who might be struggling to get to that place of victory being manifested in your marriage, to "look up" to the Lord. You can go further in your fight of faith while waiting on victory to be manifested. Like Brock, many of you are trying to give up and quit way too early. You have more gas in your tank to go further than where you are right now.

Brock crawled into the end-zone when he did not think he could make it to the fifty-yard line. Good God Almighty! He did it weighed down with Jeremy on his back. How many of you feel weighed down with the challenges of the marriage while on this path to greatness? You are not alone. Keep on moving! During the death crawl, even though the pain of it all made Brock feel as if it was impossible, his continual efforts and hard work made possible what seemed to be impossible. When it looks as if you are at the end of your rope in your marriage, even if you have to do some negotiation with your spouse or who you are in God, allow God to strengthen you so that you can keep on going. When your marriage seems as if it's beyond repair and the enemy wants you to think it's a hopeless situation, don't you give up on one another and don't you give up on God. You can go much further than you think you are capable of going. Get on your face before God. God will make sure that when you look up, you will realize that He has put a press down on the inside of you that will not allow you to give up and quit, regardless of how hard it is to keep going. Keep going even when you feel weighed down by the challenges a marriage can bring on. I am the coach that God is sending your way to encourage you to *keep going!* You will survive that which you thought was impossible. Ask me how I know. God is the same God yesterday, today, and forevermore. If He does it for me and continues to do it for me, He will do the same for you. You can, and you must survive. Brock survived, and so can you if you keep it moving by faith!

Win From Within

All of the things I have discussed in this particular chapter can be culminated by letting you know that in order to win we must "Win from Within." I want to revisit Ephesians 3:20 and I will share a different translation this time. This scripture tells us, *"Now to Him who is able to do [carry out His purpose and] do superabundantly more than all that we dare to ask or think [infinitely beyond our greatest prayers, hopes, or dreams], according to His power that is at work within us."* (AMP)

The only way we will be able to put in the hard work to make our marriages strong and healthy is to have it spring forth from within us. There is an old song we used to sing in church that says, "Something on the inside, working on the outside, oh what a change in my life!" It also says, "The Holy Ghost on the inside, working on the outside, oh what a change in my life!" Can I tell you that change comes from within? It comes from within YOU! People can encourage you, and they can inspire you. They can point you in the right direction. People can lay hands on you, anoint you with oil and speak the Word of God into your life. You can even fall out under the power of the Holy Spirit, but something has to come alive inside of you. After they have finished doing all these things, faith must come alive on the inside. If you think about the gym situation again, wanting to go to the gym to become healthy does nothing to help you become healthy if the desire has yet to move you into action. I have a coach that I once heard say, "When it comes down to motivation and activation, choose activation." He says, "Motivation can come and go. It's just like cotton candy — it tastes good for a moment, and then it's gone." I encourage you to put your faith into action so your marriage can be blessed. Allow conviction to cause your motivation to be turned into activation!

If I could touch upon Ephesians 3:20 again, I can tell you for many years, I quoted this scripture without really catching the revelation. God had to show me one day as I was reading this scripture that I was missing the key ingredient in the scripture. For many years, as a born-again believer, I allowed this scripture to go right over my head. He showed me that it was one thing to know about the power of God and another to put that power into action. It is one thing to know that God is an all-powerful God and that He is in a class all by Himself, but it is another thing to allow all that power to work on the inside of you. If you will read the scripture, it tells us that God is able to do all of these things *"ACCORDING TO"* or *"BASED ON"* what's working on the inside of us. God's Word and promises cannot and will not manifest in our lives if nothing is working inside us. Too many couples wait for a manifestation to show up while God's Word is lying dormant inside them. Faith is an action word. Earlier, when I was discussing how all the athletes were waking up early and putting their bodies through rigorous workouts, it was because they had something working on the inside of them that caused them to move beyond a desire into action so that they may win. Ms. Mary had something working inside of her. The football team had to have something to work on the inside of them to get that winning attitude because winning comes from within. With the football team, somewhere along the way, their success could no longer hinge upon their coach. The athletes' success had to move beyond their trainers' desire for them to win. They had to develop a winning attitude within themselves, because it's difficult to want and desire victory for someone more than they want it for themselves. Victory had to go further than the desire of their coach, who wanted nothing more than to see them win. Most of these athletes have a God-given gift that they had to stir up to get results. The Bible tells us to stir up the gift. Don't allow God's Word to sit dormant inside you and think that you will win! Therefore, when it comes down to succeeding in your marriage, make up your mind that you will do what seems impossible. Make up your mind that with the help of the Holy Spirit leading you and guiding you, you can, and you will go further than you ever believed or thought that you were capable of going. Marriage indeed is challenging work, but never overlook or discredit what I call "The God-factor" because, with God, all things are possible if you would only believe. God's got this!

THIS IS GOING TO GET UGLY

One Sunday afternoon, I finally had my mind made up that this would be the day that I would do what the Lord had asked me to do. My bedroom closet is not only the place where I hang my clothes, but it's also the place where I meet with God. It's the place where I have grown in leaps and bounds with my walk with God. I often take communion in the closet. I have seen many prayers answered, and the hand of God moved like never before as a result of meeting with God in my secret place.

The closet had begun getting a bit cramped and cluttered because while rushing to go to church and other functions or events, in my haste, I would fold up clothes and set them in the corner. Occasionally, clothes would fall out of the bin I had so neatly arranged onto the floor. Shoes that should have been under my bed or in my shoe rack were being stacked along the wall in the closet. I began allowing all kinds of paperwork from my job, along with notebooks that I was using to study the Word of God, to be stacked against the walls. If I can be honest, the closet had gotten out of hand. Therefore, I could no longer lie prostrate on the closet floor before the Lord in a comfortable position because either my head was touching a hanger or my feet were pushing against paperwork or a pair of shoes. Therefore, I would find myself balled up in a little space on my knees, praying and seeking God. Hey, I'm just being honest here. So, one day, the Lord spoke to me and told me to "Clean up the closet because this is the place where we meet, and it is holy ground!" He said, "This is a sacred place for us," and I agreed wholeheartedly.

After coming home from church that day, I was mentally ready to take on the task. I thought to myself that this process could not take me that long —right? So, I began picking up the clothes on the floor. I started going through the paperwork to determine what I needed to keep and what needed to be shredded or trashed. Before long, I found myself pulling neatly placed clothes off the shelves, taking clothes from the hangers to see what I wanted to keep, what needed to be thrown away, and what needed to be donated to Goodwill or another charitable organization. I thought about whether it was necessary for me to keep all the purses I had but never used. Did I want to keep the Christmas wrapping paper, gift bags, and boxes with the pretty ribbons on them for the next baby shower or the next special occasion I would attend? The closet needed some serious attention! As I started the task at hand, I found myself sitting all these things in a neat and orderly manner right outside the closet so that after I got everything out, I could come back and start setting everything up the way I wanted. I was trying my best to keep everything neat so that the outside of the closet did not begin to resemble the inside. I had a plan! But at one point, when I looked behind me, to my surprise, what started as a neatly piled stack of belongings had grown into an ugly mess. Stuff was everywhere! I said, "Oh my God, this is going to take me longer than I thought."

When I looked back at all the mess outside of the closet, God began speaking to me. He said, "Many times, this is exactly how it is in life and in marriages." God told me, "In marriage, when spouses are praying for My hand to move, when they pray, in their minds, what they're believing for is a cute little remedy or a fast and easy fix. More often than not, it is going to get ugly before it gets better." I said "Wow, Lord!" He went on to say, "Many times, it turns into a bigger mess in the natural before we see things come together and manifest spiritually!" Again, I said "Wow, that's true, Lord." I marveled at the truth as if God was telling me an untruth. But, quite frankly, I was still blown away because I have experienced that in my marriage as well as other things that I brought to God in prayer. I can recall many times after I prayed for God to move in my marriage, it seemed to get worse before it got better. I have prayed for extended periods for what appeared to be to no avail. As a believer, I know that God hears me when I pray, but sometimes delayed answers can cause you to grow weary in the wait and grow weary in well-doing. I have found myself asking God the question I once heard Joyce Meyer talk about when we desperately seek God for answers. She said that while we're waiting on God, we're constantly saying and asking God, "When, God, when?" We desire to know from God, when will you come through? Exactly when are you going to deliver God? When will this situation get better? Or, will this situation get better at all for that matter? Does that sound like any of you? But again, I had desperately prayed for deliverance while standing on the Word of God for my marriage, and before it got better, it seemed to have gotten worse. At times, it has gotten much worse. I believed that I was doing my part. I made daily confessions. I read God's Word concerning those things I believed God for in order to see the hand of God move. I found specific scriptures to put on the challenges that we were facing. My point here is that when we have prayed and when we have let our request be made known unto God, deep down inside, all we're looking for and expecting is the "Pretty" without any of the "Ugly." Am I right about it? We want the answer to come in a pretty little box wrapped up in a bow as an early birthday or Christmas gift from God. We want deliverance to come swiftly in a friendly, neat, and orderly manner minus the turbulence. We want to *go up* first without ever having to *go down* or *go through* in life and marriage. God will often allow us to experience darkness before we see daylight. The reason is that some of life's greatest lessons are taught in darkness. How can we truly know that God will bring us out unless He allows us to experience "The ugly before pretty shows up"? Having said that, I could remember one time when I was reading my Bible from Dr. Tony Evans of The Urban Alternative Ministry. As he encouraged the reader, he also said, "God often does His greatest work in the dark." It's not that God does not work in the day, but when it is the day in our lives or when we have peace from chaos, we tend to miss or ignore what God is doing because everything seems to be going well with us.

We all can agree that nobody welcomes dark days in their marriage, and I have never heard of or experienced anyone who has raised their hands to volunteer to go through the storms of life in their marriage. So again, no one likes to go through or experience dark days, but going through those tough times in marriage is inevitable. And because we cannot escape them, it behooves us to learn how to go through them and come out on the other side.

While we are waiting for God to show up, we must take on the same mindset that Daniel had in the book of *Daniel 10:12*. The angel came and told him, *"For from the first day that you set your heart on understanding this and on humbling yourself before your God, your words were heard, and I have come in response to your words."* (AMP) Even though Daniel didn't see the manifestation of the answer, he knew he was obligated to keep praying and believing God until the answer showed up. I want to spend a few moments showing you some people in the Bible where ugly showed up first, but how in the end, God was able to get the glory out of the lives of His people.

From the Pit to the Palace

Things got really ugly for Joseph before he saw better days. He had to experience dark days before the Lord raised him and blessed his life. In Genesis 37, the Bible tells us that Jacob, Joseph's father, loved him more than his other sons because Joseph was the son of his old age. And because Jacob loved Joseph more, his brothers hated him. God gave Joseph several dreams. Joseph shared those dreams with his brothers. The Bible tells us that after he shared those dreams with them, they hated him even more! God showed Joseph how he was going to reign over his brothers in one of those dreams. Can you imagine telling someone who already hates you that you will rule over them one day? You're talking about a situation going from bad to worse! They began plotting to kill Joseph. They ended up throwing Joseph into a pit to get rid of him. Then, they changed their minds and sold him to the Ishmaelites, who took him to Egypt. As you read further into this story, you will find that Joseph then ended up being sold as an enslaved person to Potiphar. Because Joseph found favor with Potiphar, he was made overseer of all that Potiphar owned. When Joseph refused Potiphar's wife's advances to sleep or to have sex with her, the ugly really got out of hand. Because he refused to sleep with her, she accused Joseph of trying to sleep with her against her will. In Potiphar's wrath, he ended up throwing Joseph into prison. God was with him every step of the way. Can you agree that chaos and confusion were rearing their ugly heads? There was nothing pretty or inviting about this whole situation. What am I saying here? God was with Joseph every step of the way. The manifestation of better days did not come until *after* he experienced many dark days at the hands of his brothers, along with Potiphar and his wife. The enemy used these people against him, BUT GOD! Isn't it good to know that while the enemy is using people to come up against you, God is using the enemy to bless you?

It is human nature to avoid confrontation and marital difficulties at all costs. I said it earlier, and I will repeat it, but I have yet to see anyone who desires to willingly be placed in stressful situations when it comes down to a marriage that seems not to be working at all, regardless of how hard you try. But, with the story I just shared about Joseph, I know that Joseph prayed his way throughout that ordeal, and I believe he was a praying man. Joseph's situation grew much worse before it got better. This story confirms that God will sometimes allow us to go into the pit before He allows us to reach the palace. He will enable you to go through difficult and ugly times before seeing better days. I encourage you to hold fast to the profession of your faith.

There is something worthy of pointing out in this story that can be found in *Genesis 50:19–20*. When his brothers feared Joseph would take vengeance upon them, he told them, *"Do not be afraid, for am I in the place of God? [Vengeance is His, not mine]. (20) As for you, you meant evil against me, but God meant it for good in order to bring about this present outcome, that many people would be kept alive [as they are this day]."* (AMP)

Joseph was telling his family that while they meant evil against him, they didn't know that God was allowing him to go through some dark days so that He could make Joseph a more incredible blessing to his family and in the lives of His people. His brothers wanted to cut Joseph's dreams short by trying to end his life, but God had another plan. God's purpose will always prevail over the plans and schemes of men and over the plan of our adversary. Many of the trials and tribulations we must endure in our marriages have the enemy written all over them. He desires to block and cut off God's will for our lives. Though the enemy means it for evil, God allows it for good. The enemy means to kill, steal, and destroy your marriage. He wants to stop vulnerable couples who can be blessed by gleaning from your marriage that it may bless their lives. He means to wreak havoc in your marriage and bring it to naught, but I am a living witness that God will use it for your good and the good of so many other struggling marriages.

The God That Sees Me

Let us take a lesson from the life of Abram, Sarai, and Hagar. God promised Abram and his wife, Sarai, a son in their old age. The promise took twenty-five years to manifest. They started speculating as to when and how God was going to bring this promise to pass. Either Sarai was convinced she could not have children, or she let anxiety get the best of her. Therefore, she spoke to Abram and asked him to go into her maidservant Hagar so the two would conceive a child. What got me about this story is that the Bible says that he listened to his wife as they both attempted to help God. As we read the story, we see that things turned really ugly, really fast for Abram, Sarai, and Hagar.

As you continue reading the story, you will see that Hagar conceived. And again, the situation went from bad to worse! I mean, it got hideous. The reason is that once Hagar conceived, the Bible says that she began looking down upon Sarai because of her infertility. Sarai became so jealous and angry that she blamed Abram for following her directions. How crazy was that? As one of my pastors would say, "She got what she wanted, but she didn't want what she got." Sarai got exactly what she wanted, but afterward, she started despising the whole situation. Abram's response to all of this craziness is found in *Genesis 16:6: "But Abram said to Sarai, 'Look, your maid is entirely in your hands and subject to your authority; do as you please with her.' So Sarai treated her harshly and humiliated her, and Hagar fled from her. (7) But the Angel of the LORD found her by a spring of water in the wilderness, on the road to [Egypt by way of] Shur. (8) And He said, 'Hagar, Sarai's maid, where did you come from and where are you going?' And she said, 'I am running away from my mistress Sarai.' (9) The Angel of the LORD said to her, 'Go back to your mistress, and submit humbly to her authority.' (10) Then the Angel of the LORD said to her, 'I will greatly multiply your descendants so that they will be too many to count.' (11) The Angel of the LORD continued,*

'Behold, you are with child, and you will bear a son; And you shall name him Ishmael (God hears), Because the LORD has heard and paid attention to your persecution (suffering).....(13) Then she called the name of the LORD who spoke to her, 'You are God Who Sees'; for she said, 'Have I not even here [in the wilderness] remained alive after seeing Him [who sees me with understanding and compassion]?' (14) Therefore the well was called Beer-lahai-roi (Well of the Living One Who Sees Me); it is between Kadesh and Bered."

God gave Abram and Sarai a promise. Once again, it took twenty-five years for the promise to manifest. Sometimes, in the process of waiting, we get tempted to go with an alternate plan. Again, the waiting will, on many occasions, tempt us to go with another plan because we believe that God is taking too long to come through. We must realize that trying to help God out and going before God can cause a lot of sorrow and heartache for everyone involved. Though this whole situation wasn't a surprise to God, God is so awesome that He still allowed everyone to be blessed. But my point here is that it got much worse before it got better. I am incredibly blessed to see how God showed up and met Hagar at the point of her need. Regardless of whether it's your marriage, your children, or your health, I believe that God always shows up in some way, shape, or form. It does not matter how bad your situation looks; God is able to flip the script.

This story about Abram, Sarai and Hagar has many moving parts. On the one hand, it's about how a couple, who had a promise from God, had to go through a rough patch before coming out on the other side. But, there is something else I want to relate to you regarding marriage is what happened to Hagar. Hagar took off and fled because of being humiliated by Sarai. She took on a "fight or flight mode." She decided to run. I am blessed to see that even at one of the lowest points in Hagar's life God met her at the point of her need. When Hagar fled to the wilderness and ran to Egypt, she could have lost her life. When the angel of the LORD showed up, she said, "You Are the God That Sees!" She went further and made it personal because she said, "Have I also here seen Him WHO SEES ME." Beer-lahai-roi means the God that lives and SEES ME. El-Roi in Hebrew also means "the God who SEES ME."

I love this story because in Genesis 16:11, the angel told Hagar that the LORD has heard and paid attention to her persecution and suffering. I want you to know that God hears you, and He is paying attention to what you are going through. What a blessing! Are you standing on a promise from God? I don't know about you, people of God, but whenever and wherever trouble arises in our lives, regardless of what area of life, isn't it good to know that we can call on "the God Who Sees?" Not only is He the God who sees, but today you can make it personal because the Bible says, "He is the God who SEES YOU!" You can put your name in there and claim that promise for your life and for your marriage because God is the same God today, yesterday, and forevermore. If He did it for Hagar, He will do the same for you. I want you to know that in your darkest hour, God hears you and pays attention to your suffering.

In verse 13, Hagar says something so profound. She says, *"Have I not even here [in the wilderness] remained alive after seeing Him [who sees me with understanding and compassion]?"* Another thing that I would like to point out in this amazing story is Hagar says that while she was in a wilderness situation, running for her life, she remained alive after seeing the God that saw her. If you want to stay alive in your wilderness situation, you have to be able to see the God who sees you. Oftentimes, when we are in what we believe to be a dark situation, many of us have a hard time seeing God. We think that God is nowhere to be found and we feel all alone. But, just like Shadrach, Meshach, and Abednego, when they were thrown into the fiery furnace, there was a fourth man in the fire with them. God wants you to know that in those difficult and challenging times, He's in the fire with us. God sees, and He knows. It makes a huge difference when we have 20/20 vision in the realm of the

Spirit, that we can see the same God who sees us and comes to our rescue. Hagar's situation let us know that while we're waiting for God to turn that ugly situation around, call on El-Roi because He hears your prayers and sees everything you're going through. God will meet you right at the point of your need.

From Caterpillar to Butterfly

I am incredibly excited to announce that my husband and I recently became first-time grandparents. I have always wanted a daughter, but God blessed us with two handsome sons. God is so fantastic at giving us the desires of our hearts. I did not personally have the girl I constantly desired, but now, I have a granddaughter. I was in love with her even before she was born. I was tremendously blessed to be in the delivery room when she arrived. It was a beautiful sight when I first laid eyes on her! I never feel like that when I see a caterpillar. I am sure it's not everybody's opinion, but they are not the prettiest little creatures I have ever laid my eyes on in this life. If I could be frank here, they are downright ugly. I am sorry, but that is my belief and I'm sticking to it. If I had to take a survey to ask you how many of you think that they are pretty, I believe that many of you would not only say that they are not the most adorable little creatures that God has created, but many of you would also say that they are kind of creepy as well.

Caterpillars start off looking one way until they begin going through a transformation process. As they are transformed, they become beautiful butterflies. Their end-stage looks so much better than their beginning stage. They start crawling before they can fly. They go through a metamorphosis. That's the process of changing a thing or person's form or nature into a completely different one by natural or supernatural means. God is always in the process of changing us by supernatural means from the person we are now to the person He has called us to be, if we're willing to participate. I know that the transformation process can be painful. I know it's not always a pretty picture but hold on, my friend. I wholeheartedly believe that God is at work doing something so awesome and so wonderful on the inside of you. I know that God loves every last one of us where we are right now, but He has called us to a higher place in Him. And as you allow God to do a work in you, your marriage will be all the more blessed as you surrender. Let that transformation process take place in your life as you continue to grow in Him while allowing God to be God.

Make Me Over Again

While we are waiting on God to manifest His promises that He has made and while we're waiting on daylight to come, it is imperative that we individually lay ourselves on the "Altar of God." As I reflect on one of those times when I was seeking God's hand to move in my marriage, as I lay there in my secret place talking to the Lord, I asked God, "What would He have me do in this particular situation?" I was pretty shocked when I heard the Lord tell me to *"Lay myself on the altar."* I thought to myself, "WHAT!!!" God was saying to me that He wanted me to have the willingness to give "ALL OF ME" so that He would have His way in my life, thereby having His way in my marriage. Too often, God cannot have His way in our marriages because we refuse to allow Him to have His way in our individual lives apart from our spouses. I always say that we're too caught up and too prone to thinking that God only wants to change our spouses. We are always praying and asking God to open *their* eyes and cause *them* to see the light of day — right? After I asked God "What would He have me to do," again, God said, "I want you to give yourself to Me right in the midst of this ugly situation. I want you to surrender right in the place of not knowing what to do." How many of you have ever been to the place to where you simply don't know what else to do? There are times outside of trying our best to obey the Word of God when we are at our wit's end. Exactly what do you do when you don't know what to do? When we don't know what to do and when we don't know which way to turn next, we are to lay ourselves on the altar of God. We are to surrender ourselves to Him and allow God to put us on the "potter's wheel!" It is only when we allow

God to put us on the potter's wheel, can He began putting His super on our natural.

I have always enjoyed reading the story in Jeremiah chapter 18. God spoke to Jeremiah and told him to go down to the potter's house, *"and there I will cause thee to hear my words."* (KJV) Did you catch that? There is always a place where God calls us to be so we can receive the blessing. If I may interject right here, I once heard that in the game of football the quarterback is not throwing the ball to the place where the receiver is, but rather, he is throwing the ball to the place where the receiver is supposed to be. The blessing will always follow obedience. So, God spoke to Jeremiah and gave him a specific area where He wanted Jeremiah to be so that he could hear His voice. Jeremiah got up and made his way to the place that was called "the potter's house" to get further instructions from God. *Jeremiah 18:3-6, reads, "Then I went down to the potter's house, and saw that he was working at the wheel. (4) But the vessel he was making from clay was spoiled by the potter's hand; so he made it over, reworking it and making it into another pot that seemed good to him. (5) Then the word of the LORD came to me: (6) "O house of Israel, can I not do with you as this potter does?" says the LORD. "Look carefully, as the clay is in the potter's hand, so are you in My hand, O house of Israel." (AMP)*

The revelation here is the quicker we come to the realization that we are individuals who are stained, tarnished, in need of continual spiritual upgrades and improvements, the better we will understand that we need God to "Make us again into another vessel," as it seems good to Him! Somebody say "Amen!" The question becomes, how badly do you want a blessed marriage? How desperate are you in wanting to be in one accord with your mate so that your marriage can be blessed and used as a tool to be a blessing to others? Our marriage can only be the recipient of the blessing of God as we make individual decisions to allow God to make us again. I have absolutely nothing to do with how God chooses to "Make Shawn again." I am not God. I cannot give Shawn a do-over in the realm of the Spirit.

However, I can lay myself on the altar and allow God to make me again if I truly desire for God to bring some comfort to chaos and elevate my faith and my trust in Him. I can let the Potter make me again as it seems good to Him and not according to what I think, how I feel about it, or according to my own specifications. The Bible says that we are marred. That means that, as individuals, we are spiritually disfigured. We are flawed, scarred, and tarnished without the help of the Potter. It pains my heart to know that we live in a society where so many people are more concerned about getting work done on their physical appearances than they are about allowing God to carry out His assignment on them spiritually. God said that we are flawed, and we must be willing to go through a metamorphosis process to be transformed.

You may be reading this book, and all you can think about is the desire to have peace in your marriage! I want to encourage you today. Your marriage may not be picture-perfect; in fact, it will never arrive at the status of perfection. But God wants you to get to that place where you can experience heaven right here on earth in your marriage when you surrender to the Potter and when you're willing to lay yourself on the Altar of God.

How many of you know that everyday life is lived in the valley or down in the trenches? As we submit ourselves to God and allow God to make us again, God will allow us to have more "Mountain-top experiences" than "Valley lows." God will allow us to experience marital bliss as we fight to stay in one accord. After thirty-one years of marriage, I am still madly in love with my husband. I never said that we have arrived and that our marriage never gets to "The ugly phase," but I sincerely love that man. He loves going to the gym and honestly does an excellent job of working hard to stay in shape. There are times when he walks by me; I still take pleasure in looking at his rear end. Yes, I do! I can admit that after being married for over thirty-one years, I still get the hots for him. *"When Out Isn't an Option"* is a book for adults, right? I'm just letting you know what is possible as you continue to trust in God.

I still feel some way when we lie in bed at night after a long exhausting day of work, and he grabs my hand before dozing off to sleep. In my spiritual imagination, that alone says to me, "Adriene, I love you." Married life should be enjoyed and not just endured. In the book of Matthew, Jesus was ministering to a rich man about his possessions. Some things that He said astonished the disciples. In *Matthew 19:26,* He said to them, *"With people [as far as it depends on them], it is impossible, but with God all things are possible."* (AMP)

Every married couple should strive to become better. I'm talking about individually and as a couple. Wherever you are right now, God wants to take you higher. Today, if your marriage is not looking too pretty, I believe with everything within me that if you willingly lay yourself on the altar of God, God will indeed bless you. If you allow the Potter to put you on the Potter's Wheel and make you again, a metamorphosis process will begin to take place because you have allowed Him to do what seems best to the Potter.

Revelation 12:11 says, "And they overcame and conquered him because of the blood of the Lamb and because of the word of their testimony...." (AMP)

God significantly uses the words of our testimony to bless others. We have a testimony that can set the captives free.

Other people need to know how God has helped you come out victoriously and not just leave you as the victim. Tests should always give us testimonies! I never would have had the privilege and the opportunity to share with you, had I not seen God use my marriage for good to save many people alive!

I speak and declare that "Your marriage will also overcome every attack. It will outlive and overcome every scheme, every device of trickery and every strategy that has been strategically formed to destroy your marriage. I bind up every plot that has been launched at your marriage for the sole purpose of causing it to disintegrate and I speak and say that IT WON'T WORK! You are overcomers. Yes, there will be times that it will get ugly before it gets better, but I declare and decree that your marriage will stand the test of time. You shall be a witness and a testimony of what the power of God is able to do in the lives of married couples that allow God to make them again! You will not give up and you will not give in because God is not through blessing you.

My husband and I are overcomers. We have not arrived, but by faith, as we continue to trust in the LORD with all of our hearts and lean not to our own understanding, we will continue to experience victory! And so can you!

THIS MEANS WAR!

"If you ever want to know how much you really love the LORD, get married!" Those were the words of our marriage counselor as my husband and I sat on the sofa one beautiful Saturday morning. I believe the marriage counselor knew that in marriage, couples encounter some serious spiritual warfare!

Whatever stage you're in on your marriage journey, I believe that by now, as a believer, you have realized that you have enlisted in the "Army of the LORD." Hopefully, by now, you have also learned that you have an opponent who wants to see you go down and take you out of the fight by any means necessary. And anyone who has enlisted in the LORD'S Army must constantly stand on guard.

There is a song that I really love that was written by Pastor Charles Jenkins on his CD entitled "Any Given Sunday." That song inspired this particular chapter, and the name of the song is "THIS MEANS WAR."

If you have never listened to that song, it is imperative that you take some time to listen to it, especially if you are in the midst of a severe battle in your marriage. If you're having a family crisis, if you need healing in your body, or if your children appear to have gone wild, you must listen to this song.

Pastor Jenkins was an invited guest at a church in Nashville, Tennessee. And before he started to sing this song at the church gathering that day, he began by saying, "Whatever you're facing, whether it's an obstacle, opportunity, or opposition, there will be times that we want to *break down, fall down,* or *go down.*" He says, "In life, we can be overwhelmed, but we have to learn how to bear down."

I am in total agreement with Pastor Jenkins. We must learn how to say, "No weapon that is formed against us shall be able to prosper. I can do all things through Christ that gives me strength." I tell you that this song has gotten me through many dark days in my marriage and many lonely and sleepless nights. It lifted my spirits when the enemy barged his way into my home, invited and uninvited. Let's be honest here because sometimes, we play a massive role in inviting enemies into our homes and lives. As I previously stated, in the words of Tom Bodett in the Motel 6 commercial, we leave the light on for the enemy, and he shows up without fail. Again, this song has helped me when the adversary has tried, and many times has succeeded on many occasions in wreaking havoc and sowing seeds of strife, division, and discord in my marriage. And because of such, it forced me into declaring war! We can sit around and keep crying and complaining or go to war!

Soldiers who are at war already know that they have an enemy. Therefore, they are not laid back and unconcerned about the battle at hand while on the battlefield. They're not acting and behaving as if they're not in a battle zone, but they are cautious, watchful, and alert. And regardless of whether we declare war on the enemy or not, it doesn't prevent him from declaring war on us. He will attack whether we're ready or not. Remember 1 *Peter 5:8-10 says, "Be sober [well balanced and self-disciplined], be alert and cautious at all times. That enemy of yours, the devil, prowls around like a roaring lion [fiercely hungry], seeking someone to devour. (9) But resist him, be firm in your faith [against his attack— rooted, established, immovable], knowing that the same experiences of suffering are being experienced by your brothers and sisters throughout the world. [You do not suffer alone.] (10) After you have suffered for a little while, the God of all grace [who imparts His blessing and favor], who called you to His own eternal glory in Christ, will Himself complete, confirm, strengthen, and establish you [making you what you ought to be]."* (AMP)

God warns us by letting us know that we must be sober. We must be clearheaded. We must be of a sound mind. Make sure that you are always alert and watchful because our adversary loves to strike when we least expect him to launch an attack. The Bible lets us know that being in war also means some suffering will be involved. There will be prisoners of war who the enemy holds captive. There will be some casualties of war. A casualty of war is not limited to a death, but it is a military person who can be wounded, injured, sick, missing in action or captured by the enemy. Therefore, we must not be ignorant of the battle that we are facing. Our human nature runs from suffering at every turn. The Word of God tells us that after we have suffered a little while, God Himself will indeed come and strengthen us. While you're waiting on God in the heat of the battle, continue speaking God's Word. There is always a specific word that we can declare and decree for every problem and for every attack that will cause victory to show up. It often takes the enemy to show up one too many times in our marriage, in our bedrooms, or through another lousy argument for some of us to declare war. Oftentimes, it takes us to get so tired of being on the receiving end of a marital attack for us to say "ENOUGH."

<u>ENOUGH</u>

How many of you have ever seen the movie "Enough" with Jennifer Lopez? As you can see, I love using movies for analogies because they are great tools to teach us God's Word. For those of you who haven't watched the movie enough, let's take a look into the details of what pushed her over the edge and forced her to declare war on the enemy, which was her very own husband. In this movie, she plays a terrified and battered wife. She had a charming daughter whom she loved very much. No amount of submissiveness on her part kept her abusive husband from beating her. So, fearing for her life, she decided to take boxing lessons to defend herself. Her instructor, of course, taught her how to fight back. He taught her how to protect herself and how to take down that combative and abusive spirit. He taught her how to stop sitting there being the victim while learning how to be victorious. And when her lessons were complete, and after she built up her confidence, she was ready to declare war! At that point, she was no longer on the defense but got on the offense and *sought him out*. Even though she was very apprehensive about taking him on, she did it anyway because she knew what was at stake. She called him out on the carpet. Not only did she declare war, but she was victorious over the enemy. She took down the enemy. We must always find ways through God's word to place ourselves in the position to win in marriage. I don't know about you, but I don't particularly appreciate sitting around licking my wounds.

We might have been traumatized and victimized, but we definitely don't have to keep playing the victim. We can shout hallelujah to that because we are victorious in Christ Jesus. God has already given us victory. And because He has already given us the win, we must stop seeking, searching, and looking for victory. We already have it. We're only waiting for the promise to show up and manifest in the natural. Therefore, stop fighting in hopes of gaining victory, take God's word, and learn how to fight *from* your place of victory! That takes faith, and we have to learn how to fight the good fight of faith. We must be aware of the fact that there are some fights that we must fight that are considered to be "A GOOD FIGHT."

The Apostle Paul tells Timothy, his son in the ministry, in *1 Timothy 6:12 to fight the good fight of faith.* I know it sounds like an oxymoron. Right now, somebody may be trying to figure out why God coupled the word "Good" with the word "fight?" Yet, God calls it a good fight. All fights aren't considered to be good fights. Many people are fighting fights that do not have any reward attached to them whatsoever. Thank God that the good fight of faith has lasting rewards. Just like Jennifer Lopez, if you never come to the place in the heat of the battle where you can say "ENOUGH," the enemy will keep making you think that you're the victim. He will keep making you feel like there is no possible way you can win out over his attacks. He'll keep telling you that you are defeated and that there is no possible way to walk in victory. The Bible says that the devil is the father of lies. Jennifer's husband in this movie was so used to her sitting in the corner and shaking in her boots that he never thought she could or would dare try to take him on. He assumed she would always be a prisoner of war, held firmly in his grips. But she took him on, and she took him down simply because she was courageous enough to declare war!

I can hear somebody saying, "So what exactly does it mean to declare war on the enemy — what does that look like?" You might even be wondering and asking yourself, "Do I have what it takes to declare war?" You're asking yourself, "What are the eligibility requirements to participate? And at what point in my life or my walk with God must I declare war?" Declaring war means that you're willing to take God's Word and use the Word of God as an instrument and as a weapon over your opponent. When we declare war, we're proclaiming that we will no longer express ourselves as the loser by accepting defeat. In other words, we are making it known that "We are in it to win it!"

Every born-again believer has been given the spiritual authority to use God's Word as a weapon. God desires that we declare war on our opponent on an as-needed basis. You declare war when you're in the heat of the battle. As a matter of fact, we should be confessing God's Word over our marriages and our lives every day as a way of living. We should constantly speak God's Word into the atmosphere because the Word of God is alive, and it is active. Are you using the Word as an instrument of war? The first part of *Hebrews 4:12* says, *"For the word of God is living and active and full of power [making it operative, energizing, and effective]. It is sharper than any two-edged sword."* (AMP) I don't know about you, but I am rejoicing just reading this scripture. Again, the scripture says that God's Word is a living Word that is operative, energizing, and effective! Good God Almighty! It is mandatory for a child of God to declare war. Who wants to keep being a constant pushover in the realm of the Spirit and prey to the forces of darkness?

I really want to make it practical for you. First and foremost, to declare war, you must dress the part. You must dress for success because victory has a specific dress code attached to it that you must abide by if you want to walk in victory instead of staring at it afar off. If you are not walking in victory right now in your marriage, maybe it's because you're not appropriately dressed. Make no mistake about it — we cannot walk in victory if we are underdressed for battle. I'm not speaking about a three-piece suit or your favorite dress hanging in your closet. The adversary doesn't care anything about what you look like on the outside as long as the inside stays in a state of confusion and chaos. What concerns him the most is that you never get to the place in life, where something on the inside begins to bring about a real change on the inside of you. You have to have on the proper attire if you're going to be successful in fighting for what rightly belongs to you. Therefore, you must put on *"The Whole Armor of God!"*

God has given us some battle gear when we declare war, and He has given us some weaponry to suit up with while we're in warfare. Never attempt to declare war and go into battle or on the battlefield naked or half-dressed. Always remember the battle plays out in our minds even as it plays out in the natural realm. Every last one of us has lost spiritual battles trying to show up for war without being dressed in the proper attire.

Ephesians chapter six gives us a very detailed list of weaponry we must use. *Ephesians 6:11–18 says, "Put on the whole armor of God, that ye may be able to stand against the wiles of the devil. For we wrestle not against flesh and blood, but against principalities, against powers, against the rulers of the darkness of this world, against spiritual wickedness in high places. Wherefore take unto you the whole armor of God, that ye may be able to withstand in the evil day, and having done all, to stand. Stand therefore, having your loins girt about with truth, and having on the breastplate of righteousness; And your feet shod with the preparation of the gospel of peace; Above all, taking the shield of faith, wherewith ye shall be able to quench all the fiery darts of the wicked. And take the helmet of salvation, and the sword of the Spirit, which is the word of God: Praying always with all prayer and supplication in the Spirit and watching thereunto with all perseverance and supplication for all saints...."* (KJV)

When I read this list of weaponry that God has given us to dress for success, I am convinced that no one in their right mind would ever think about going outdoors with a fur coat on in 105-degree temperatures. And likewise, no one in their right mind would ever go outside in a tank top in 30 degrees below zero temperatures during a snowstorm.

Ephesians 6:11–18 is our battle-gear Saints of God, and it's how we dress for battle. We must never leave home without it. In addition to that, we have to be very careful about becoming over-relaxed and underdressed in our homes with our spouses. Just in case you didn't know it, or if you require a reminder, oftentimes, the most-fierce battles have a way of taking place right under our own roofs. I am fully aware that conflict occurs with co-workers, church folk, family, and friends alike. But, the most intense battles often occur right in our homes with our spouses. Major warfare plays out in our homes because we tend to put down our armor around our spouses because of familiarity and becoming too comfortable instead of staying watchful and alert. We have developed a tendency to say to ourselves, "Oh, that's just Adriene," or "that's just Shawn." We relax spiritually, not knowing that's the very place where the enemy is looking to strike first. Our marriage is the place where he's planning and plotting to attack first. He knows that's the very place that will do the most damage and cause the greatest heartache. So, because of this truth, our homes are the place where we must constantly be on guard. Satan cannot stand godly marriages. He despises it in a way that I don't think our finite minds can fully comprehend. *Matthew 10:36* further explains why we should stand on guard in our homes. It says *"A man's foes shall be they of his own household."* That same scripture in the Message Bible says, *"Well-meaning family members can be your worst enemies."* Now, that's really something to pause and think about right there. When we think about how well-meaning family members and members of our own household can be our worst enemy, that alone can be very disheartening.

I would be remiss if I didn't mention that in the movie "ENOUGH" that even though Jennifer Lopez declared war on her husband, I want you to know that we are not wrestling against flesh and blood in our marriage. Her husband was indeed her enemy in the movie. Still, in real life, we are sometimes deceived into thinking, during times of arguments and disagreements, that our spouses are actually the real enemy. Our spouses are not our enemies, and vice versa. Know that regardless of how much or how bad we hurt one another, we are not each other's enemies. Therefore, let's not treat each other as such, lest we find ourselves waging war against the wrong person. Again, this is not a flesh and blood battle. As the scripture states, we are wrestling against principalities, against powers, against the rulers of the darkness of this world, and against spiritual wickedness in high places. Always keep that top of mind during an argument or when declaring war.

How many of you know that the adversary is excellent and cunning at throwing the rock and hiding his hand? Be on guard and watch out for his many schemes, tricks, and devices. *2 Corinthians 2:11 tells us that the enemy is able to get an advantage of us if we are ignorant of his devices.* A device is considered to be something that is made or adapted for a particular purpose. It can also be a ploy, a plot, a scheme, a cunning plan, or a trick. And in these days of the COVID-19 pandemic with people having to deal with life differently, for many, short tempers and animosity are prevalent. If we're not careful, anything can be turned into a device in a marriage that comes straight from the hand of the enemy. Remember the Bible says our adversary is walking about seeking whom he may devour. Don't let it be your marriage!

It's On!

I recall one time that my husband and I were having a severe battle being played out in our marriage. Of course, it was the enemy, yet we were guilty of pointing our fingers at one another. I can say that this was one of those times that I was really knocked down in the realm of the Spirit. I lay in my bed for several days flicking through television channels while battling the spirit of depression. I'm telling you, I literally felt as if the enemy had upper-cut me. I was one hundred percent sure of the fact that He was hitting us below the belt. By now, I'm sure you know that he doesn't believe in fighting fair at all. I was so angry and broken that I had the nerve to have an attitude with God. In the midst of my going through all of this pain and heartache, the First Lady of the ministry where we were attending church called me and asked me to minister to the ladies one night.

She wanted me to share the Word of God precisely one week from the time she called. I said, "God, you have got to be kidding me. Are you serious right now?" I am convinced that God has a sense of humor. I felt like God was determined to get me out of that funk by any means necessary. So, quite naturally, the invitation forced me to get up and stop feeling sorry for myself. I must admit that this was one trial I allowed to have me sitting around licking my wounds. But, this call forced me to find my way back into my prayer closet to seek God as to what He would have me minister to His daughters. If I was going to be able to hear from God as I needed to, I had one week to dry up my tears and prostrate myself before the Lord. I had one week to kiss the spirit of depression goodbye and say good riddance to the pity party to which I was obviously invited. In other words, I had one week to prepare myself for what God had ordained. I knew the invitation was from God, so I couldn't refuse the invitation as my flesh wanted me to do. So, the Lord, who is always very faithful, spoke to me and told me to show up at church that night, all dressed up in army fatigue. He instructed me to dress for battle. He wanted me to show up looking on the outside like what I had been experiencing and going through on the inside. The problem was-I didn't have anything that resembled or even looked like army fatigues in my house. So, I began calling around to different people. "Hey, do you have some army boots I can use?" I continued calling. "Hey, would you happen to have army pants and an army jacket that I could borrow?" I kept calling. "Would you happen to have a hat that I could use?"

Before I knew it, I had everything I needed because I was specifically instructed to dress the part. Can I tell you, my friend, I showed up at church that night with an attitude? I wasn't mad at my husband, and I wasn't angry at the people of God, but I was mad as hell at the enemy. As I ministered that night, the power of the Holy Spirit showed up and showed out. The women of God were delivered from some things they were going through, not only because I said, "yes" to God, but also because I decided to get up and say "ENOUGH." God showed up that night in such a powerful way. I knew in my heart of hearts that I had to get up, stop feeling sorry for myself, and go to war!

God wanted to show me that it wasn't just about me. We must know that many of the things we go through are for somebody else's deliverance as well as our own. You need to know that the attack isn't just on you or about you. Are you hearing me? The enemy wants to touch the lives of those who are connected to you when he attacks you. Once again, God knows how to flip the script. When we know and understand that God is in the midst, and it was God who allowed it in the first place, we can better understand the reason we can call it "a good fight." God intends for some good to spring forth out of a messy and ugly situation.

I came out of that battle with my hands up, and someone else's life was touched for the better, only after I decided to go to war. One thing I learned during that battle is that getting knocked down is okay, but don't stay down. Get back up again. Get up, dust yourself off, and get back into the fight. Being knocked down doesn't mean you are knocked out. I understand that there will be times when the battle will have us feeling spiritually deflated. The word "deflated" means having a sudden loss of confidence or optimism.

It can also mean to have the feeling as if you've gotten all the wind knocked out of you. So yes, sometimes we will lose faith and begin thinking or saying to ourselves, "Can or will this marriage ever get better?" I speak and say, "Yes, it can!" But can I also tell you that being deflated or losing confidence and optimism doesn't mean you have been defeated. Being deflated does not have to disqualify you from getting back up again and walking in victory unless we allow it to do so. That's a trick of the enemy. He wants you to keep looking down. He wants you to keep acting, thinking, talking, and feeling down. When your marriage is under attack, it becomes all about perception. It's all about how you allow your mind to process the challenge that is at hand. *Proverbs 23:7 says, "For as he thinketh in his heart, so is he."* (KJV) When under attack, many times, the problem is that you haven't developed a righteous indignation against the enemy. You haven't gotten mad enough to do something about what the enemy is doing in your life and marriage. I'm not talking about being mad enough by continuing to operate in the flesh or by doing something crazy that's outside of God's will. I'm not talking about breaking your spouse's windows on their vehicles or flattening their tires. I'm speaking about being mad enough to declare war on the forces of darkness who are trying to destroy your marriage. Stop allowing the enemy to think he has left you for dead because you refuse to fight the good fight of faith. GET UP! Sometimes, God allows the enemy to push us around so we can finally roll up our sleeves and fight. I said it earlier and I will say it again. Somebody who is reading even now, your marriage feels as if it has been placed on a life-support system. It seems as if it's kind of touch-and-go right now. Some of you honestly don't know if your marriage is going to survive through the night or ever see the light of day. The enemy is hoping that you will pull the plug and say, "Ashes to ashes and dust to dust." Just as at the gravesite, he wants you to say your final goodbyes and walk away mourning. I declare and decree that your marriage shall live and not die.

If God didn't give you a biblical way out, who are you to pull the plug and call it quits? Draw a line in the sand and decide that you will stand your ground! Take on the mindset of Job. The latter part of *Job 14:14*, He said, *"I will wait all the days of my struggle until my change and release will come."* (AMP) When it seemed as if he had nothing left to fight for, he came to the end of himself, opened up his mouth, and said, "I will wait on God and keep on standing until change shows up." Job waited for a change to come.

Teach My Hands to War

Psalms 144:1 says, "Blessed be the LORD, my Rock, and *my great strength, who trains my hands for war and my fingers for battle...."* (AMP) David was letting us know that God taught him how to fight and ultimately helped him win. Always consult God in what He would have you do in battle. God, on many occasions, will instruct us on how to fight and what we must do for victory to manifest. He has many ways to bless, heal, and deliver us. In the Bible, when it came down to healing, He was able to "speak the word only," and the centurion was healed. He told someone else to go and dip in the pool while He rubbed spit into someone else's eye to receive healing and deliverance. When everything was said and done, they all received healing. God is the one who will teach your hands to war. As you seek His face in a place of intimacy, He will instruct you as He teaches you how to war a good warfare. If you are a child of the Most-High God, you have what it takes. If you have the Spirit of God living on the inside, that's your assurance that you have what it takes to win. Stir up the Spirit of God. Stir up your faith. Stop allowing the enemy to referee your life. God has already given us the winning strategy. It's all in the B I B L E!

I want to encourage you by saying that the same power that raised Christ from the dead also dwells in you. And greater is He who is you than he who is in the world. I have made up my mind that I will continue to fight for my marriage. How about you? Marriage is not for the faint at heart. Whoever said this fight would be easy? It's not easy, but God said we have the victory! Know that there will be times that fighting the good fight of faith will require you to march right into the enemy's camp and take back what rightfully belongs to you. Take your peace back. Take your joy back. Some of you must go into the enemy's camp and take your marriage back. Because I believe that, in every marriage, there will be plenty of times that we must be willing to draw a line in the sand and declare to the enemy "This Means War!"

WHO DO I SAY THAT I AM

I can remember as clearly as day how I was so down and out some years after we got married. We had purchased our first home to live in, which was a two-bedroom townhouse, precisely three months after having our first son Caleb. Becoming a mom brought me great joy and happiness. I tell you, I was so happy not only to be a mom, but also to have a home to call my own. We lived in an apartment complex before purchasing our house, which was still very nice. About one and a half years later, we tried to have another baby, but we lost three babies back-to-back due to me having what the doctors called "A rare blood type." I must say that I had a great gynecologist in my child-bearing years. After my third miscarriage, with much prayer and some medical intervention, I was able to give birth to my second son Joshua. We call them the "Faith Team." From the very beginning, my husband and I raised our children in church and tried our best to instill God's Word in them to give them a good spiritual foundation.

About four years after marriage, my husband and I had a terrible argument. I spent days sobbing and wishing to see better days. I recall many days and nights wetting my pillow, wanting to make up, but both of us were too prideful to be the first to apologize. I'm sure many of you can say amen to that. So, one night, while on my knees in my living room, as I was crying out to God for deliverance from all of the strife and discord we were experiencing, God spoke to me. God is so wonderful and so awesome. While I was right there on my knees, He said, "Adriene, I know you are hurting right now. Even in the midst of your tears and pain — can you praise Me anyhow?" That night, somehow, I was able to muster up enough strength and enough faith to praise my heavenly Father as He asked me to do. In this lesson, I believe God was teaching me to walk by faith and not by my emotions. He was teaching me that praise was an instrument of war. At this time, I had been saved for about four years. He showed me that praise brings about deliverance and how He inhabits the praises of His people. God was letting me know in His presence I could experience the fullness of joy. I was learning how to acquire peace and joy in the Holy Ghost. Catch that, somebody! I went to bed that night feeling a little better, but still feeling very broken-hearted and shattered. That was a Saturday night.

The following day, it was time to get up and make our way to the Sunday morning service. As I was standing in the mirror looking at myself, somewhere in the middle of putting on my eyeliner and lipstick, the Spirit of the LORD started to speak to me again. This time, God said to me, "Take a good look at yourself." As I stood there looking very intently at myself in the mirror while crying all over my make-up job again, God asked me, "Do you know who you are?"

Immediately, God brought the scripture to me found in *Mark 8:27–30* when Jesus asked the disciples, *"Who do men say that I am?"* And they answered and said, *"Some say, John the Baptist, and others say, Elijah, while others say one of the prophets."* Jesus cut to the chase and asked, "Who do you say that I am?" Peter said, *"You are Christ."* Jesus says, *"Peter, flesh and blood did not reveal that to you but my Father in heaven."* (paraphrased)

Can I testify to the fact that in an instant, all of the sadness was gone from me? All of a sudden, I could feel the presence of the Lord coming upon me and rising up big on the inside of me. It was like a breath of fresh air. It was at that time that God had me ask myself this question: I said, "WHO DO I SAY THAT I AM?" That was one of many turning points in my marriage because we never arrived, but we continued to grow. Then God began to show me that it's okay for the pastor or minister to slap some anointing oil on me and declare and decree victory on my behalf. He showed me that it's okay for someone to prophesy and give us scripture after scripture, trying to tell us who we are in God. Until you and I get to the place in our lives where we know beyond a shadow of a doubt who we are, we will stay down and out. When we don't know who we are in God, the Word of God and the encouragement we receive from others will come into one ear and go right back out the other ear. It's because the Word of God, the encouragement, and all of the edification we receive have no place to land. The Word of God has no anchor to grab hold of that will cause it to make a real difference in our lives in order to help us to stand. It's like the story in the Bible that talks about how the Sower went forth to sow some seeds. Some seeds fell on good ground. Some seeds fell on stony ground, and some fell on shaky ground. In life, in some places where the seed of the Word of God lands, it just sits on the outer surface of our hearts. It never penetrates and goes deep enough to take root so that it may grow and produce a harvest. When this happens, the enemy comes and snatches away the little we have heard. The good news is that God is able to allow His Word to fall on good ground. I'm praying that this very word you are hearing right now is falling on good ground and it will bring forth a harvest that will alter the course of your life. Knowing who we are and whose we are in God changes everything in our lives and our marriages.

When God was speaking to me, letting me know who I am, as He was prompting me to ask myself the question, "Who do I say I am?" I had previously accepted my calling as a gospel minister. And don't think for a moment that pastors, preachers, elders, and ministers don't go through. *Psalms 34* says, *"Many hardships and perplexing circumstances confront the righteous, But the LORD rescues him from them all."* (AMP) That's good news because if you are righteous, you will go through. So, my pastor, at that time, used to allow the newly unlicensed ministers to go forth with a fifteen-minute sermon right before Bible study every week. He allowed us to exercise our preaching and teaching gift or lack thereof. It wasn't too long after that major attack from the enemy that it was my turn to share God's word before Bible study. And guess what my topic was? If you said, "WHO DO I SAY THAT I AM?" you're exactly right. And, if I can say so, I preached my heart out that night. I believed it was because I had some righteous indignation against the enemy!

It takes the Spirit of God to show us who we are in God. As children of the Most-High God, we should always be in the process of cultivating our spiritual lives before the LORD. It helps for the greater good in growing spiritually, in life, as a person, and in a marriage. Knowing who we are and whose we are helps God to stand up and rise up big on the inside of us to meet every challenge we face.

One day while ministering to a close friend of mine, the LORD had me speak into her life. God told me to tell her the words "Stop doubting who you are in God and who God is in you!" Now that's huge! Too often, we doubt and reason away who we are in God and who God is IN US! By the way, that nugget isn't just for my friend. As I think about it, any growing believer can get in on this nugget of truth because the enemy is always working overtime trying to convince us that we are not who God says we are! Open your mouth and say, "I am who God says I am. I can do what

God says I can do. And I can have what God says I can have!" PERIOD! God tells us we can do ALL THINGS THROUGH CHRIST as He strengthens us.

Once again, the Word of the Lord tells us to build ourselves up on our most holy faith. We will never know who we are in God if we don't take the time out of our busy schedules and get into God's presence to build ourselves up. My friend, there are some reinforcements in the Word of God that we'll have to put in place to aid us and help us on the path of knowing who we are in God. If we're going to know who we are in God and who God is in us, listen, we have to be instrumental in working with the Spirit of God to help us to go on to "next," while refusing to be stuck and stagnated! I want you to know that God has equipped us with everything we need to build OURSELVES UP so that we can stand and wait patiently on God concerning our marriages. When God tells us to "build ourselves up," one thing that He is trying to convey to us is we must stop waiting for someone else to do what God has given us and equipped us to do for ourselves. I thank God for pastors. I, too, am a pastor. I absolutely love ministering the Word of God to others. I love seeing the power of God move in people's lives. But, there should come a time in all of our lives when we ourselves must know how to rise to the occasion as believers.

You have to rise up and come to a place where you know and believe that the same power and the same anointing that God is using a man or woman of God to speak into your life, you too have that same spiritual authority and that same power if you believe it. The same way you have the power, authority, and ability to turn the thermostat up or down in your home to adjust the temperature is the same way God expects you and me to operate in that same authority in the realm of the Spirit to change the atmosphere in your marriage. You have to use it! The power of God can't just lie dormant inside of you. You're going to have to know how to get alone with God and pull on the power of the Holy Ghost to pull yourself up out of the muck and the mire when it comes down to fighting for your marriage. David said in the Word of God that he had to know how to ENCOURAGE HIMSELF in the Lord. Marriage is not a sprint. Building a strong, healthy, and lasting marriage is a marathon.

You don't get there overnight. It takes time. Successful marriages take practice and consistency. Something else that it takes is much trial and error and much forgiveness. Every day, be willing to put in the effort because blessed marriages don't just happen. It's disheartening to say, but contrary to popular belief, couples do end up "getting out" of marriages, even when they still love each other very much. I know couples who have gotten divorced who truly still loved each other while signing the divorce papers. I want you to hear my heart here. It behooves us to take advantage of every opportunity to build ourselves up so we can stand when everything else in us is screaming to cut our losses and let it go! God created and designed marriage to be for keeps! Therefore, don't take each other for granted!

If the Lord says the same, my husband and I are embarking upon celebrating thirty-two years of marriage soon. What a milestone! That's a significant accomplishment for me. To God be all the glory. I take no credit for it outside of trying my best to stand on the Word of God and the promises of God that cannot fail. I do my best to hold fast to the profession of my faith without wavering. In demanding and challenging times, I keep reaching beyond the breaking point even when I feel stretched out like a rubber band that is about to pop at any moment. It's the LORD'S doing. Somebody, you may be struggling right now in your marriage. Can I encourage you to reach beyond the breaking point? Don't give up, and don't give in because God is not done blessing your marriage.

You have too many lives to touch. God does not want us to waste our pain. God uses that pain and heartache to teach us and to show us how strong and powerful we are. He uses it to show us who we are in Him and who He is in us. Use that pain to bless another couple contemplating calling it quits. Use every trial and heartache to thrust you to another level of faith. Know that God designs our misery to turn right back around to become our ministry. I am so adamant about not wasting my pain. *2 Corinthians 1:3–4* says, *"Blessed [gratefully praised and adored] be the God and Father of our Lord Jesus Christ, the Father of mercies and the God of all comfort, (4) who comforts and encourages us in every trouble so that we will be able to comfort and encourage those who are in any kind of trouble, with the comfort with which we ourselves are comforted by God."* (AMP)

God wants us to use the same comfort that we have received from Him in times of trouble and grief to turn right back around and comfort others with the same comfort we have received from the Father. With a grateful heart, this is why I have finally said "yes" to God in writing this book. God has been too good, kind, and merciful to me in my marriage to keep quiet.

<u>Little Johnnie</u>

I heard a story when I first became a born-again believer. This story has blessed my life throughout the years when I think about what I choose to magnify. I want to share this story with you, because once again, knowing who we are in God has everything to do with our perception. Our perception is the way that we see things. It's the way that we grasp, observe, and understand things. Therefore, we must be aware of the fact that our perception is our reality, whether it's right or wrong. And the way that we perceive things is the very lens through which we will live out our lives. It has been said that some people see the glass as half empty while others see the glass as half full. It's all how you're looking at it. So, the story about little Johnnie is about a little boy who loved playing outside with his friends after school. Every day when Little Johnnie's dad came home, he was sure to find his son playing outside with his friends. So, one day, when Little Johnnie's dad came home from work, to his surprise, his son was sitting inside with a very sad countenance. Little Johnnie was sitting in the window seat, looking outside, and crying as he watched all his friends doing what he so loved doing, which was playing outside. His dad asked, "Little Johnnie, why are you sitting inside? Why aren't you outside playing with your friends? And what are you doing with that magnifying glass in your hands turned the wrong way?" His dad went on to say, "You're supposed to be looking out of the magnifying glass so that you could see things bigger than what they really are." Little Johnnie looked up at his dad with tears running down his face and said, "Dad, there's a guy out there who's always picking on me. I'm looking through this magnifying glass the opposite way because I want to be able to see him smaller than what he really is!" This story has and continues to bless me when the enemy comes along and tries to "Pick on" my marriage. I often think about this story when the adversary tries to pick at our thoughts as he goes about in his efforts to tear our marriage apart. It is in those times, through the grace of God that I desperately try to look through the lens of the Word of God so I can see the adversary smaller than what he really is. As we strive to build a strong and healthy marriage, we will always have an enemy picking on us. We will always have an enemy trying to cause strife, division, confusion, and chaos. God wants us to be able to flip the script. That's the time that we have to start looking at and seeing the situation differently from how the enemy desires us to see it. That's the time that we must begin magnifying the LORD.

God wants us to look at every situation and circumstance in a way that will magnify Him as opposed to magnifying the problem or the enemy. The psalmist says in *Psalms 34:3, "O Magnify the LORD with me and let us lift up His name together."* (AMP) When trouble comes knocking, remember it's all about our spiritual perception, and it's all about how we decide to look at it because our perception will always be our reality. Never forget who you are in God and who God is in you! Allow God to rise up big on the inside of you! So, may I ask you, "Who Do You Say You Are?"

WHAT'S LOVE GOT TO DO WITH IT?

"You must understand how the touch of your hand makes my pulse react. That it's only the thrill of boy meetin' girl —opposites attract. It's physical — Only logical — You must try to ignore that it means more than that! Oh oh, what's love got to do, got to do with it? What's love but a second-hand emotion? What's love got to do, got to do with it? Who needs a heart when a heart can be broken?"

Those are the words recorded and released in the song written by Terry Britten and Graham Lyle, sung by the legendary Tina Turner in 1984. The song is entitled "What's Love Got to Do with It."

It goes without saying that Tina Turner has experienced a broken heart. It also goes without saying that somewhere along the way in marriage, you, too, will experience a broken heart. It's inevitable. It's unavoidable. It doesn't matter how much your spouse gives you butterflies when they kiss you or how often they respond to your love language. There is absolutely no way around having our hearts broken in relationships. So, if broken hearts are a part of the marriage relationship, I believe it's essential for two people to learn how to love each other —God's-style. How many of you would agree with me that the three words "I love you" are thrown around very loosely these days? They can be yet so significant in special moments, while also, at the same time, they can mean so little, based upon who's speaking them at the time they are being spoken. They have become words that so many people use because they've gotten so used to saying them without having real meaning behind them. There have been plenty of spouses that have heard the words "I love you" countless times only to find out that their spouses have committed adultery. Spouses have listened to "I love you" from mates while experiencing physical, verbal, or emotional abuse, which I will discuss later. I am under the conviction that married couples would have happier and healthier relationships if they would pattern their love toward each other according to how God defines love. If I had to answer Tina Turner's question, when it comes down to marriage, love has everything to do with it. It matters to those who seek to have a marriage that God truly blesses. *Galatians 5:6* tells us that faith is activated and expresses itself through love.

In other words, faith works by love. A genuine faith cannot be operable if love is missing. I'm sure you know that when you are reading the ingredients on a product you have purchased, whatever element has the most considerable amount in the product will be listed first on the label. For example, if you buy a box of candy from the store, even though the candy has other ingredients, sugar will likely be the first ingredient listed on the label. That means that it has more sugar than anything else in the candy. And when it comes down to marriage, love should be the main ingredient according to the Word "God." God has given every born-again believer fruit that we should display on a daily basis in our marriage. I want to turn your attention to

Galatians chapter five. As we read this scripture, I want you to pay special attention to the fact that when God says the fruit of the Spirit, He does not say *"The fruits of the Spirit."* Even though the fruit of the Spirit has different and distinct characteristics, all of the characteristics, as a whole, are still defined as one fruit. It's comparable to the Trinity. We have the Father, the Son, and the Holy Ghost; they are three, yet they are one. So, when it comes down to the fruit of the Spirit, all of the individual characteristics spring forth from one root. And that root is love. So, God gives us the wherewithal to operate in all capacities of the fruit. Therefore, if we can operate in one, we can operate in all of them if we choose to do so. *Galatians 5:22–23, says "But the fruit of the Spirit [the result of His presence within us] is love [unselfish concern for others], joy [inner peace], patience [not the ability to wait, but how we act while waiting], kindness, goodness, faithfulness, gentleness, self-control. Against such things, there is no law."*

That is the fruit of the Spirit that we should operate in daily. Did you notice what fruit appeared first as Galatians lists the individual characteristics of the fruit? Love appeared first. "Why is it?" somebody might be asking. It's because when it comes down to the fruit of the Spirit, again, love is the main ingredient, and rightfully so. If we operate in love the way God meant for us to do so, we will have absolutely no problem flowing in every other fruit though they are one fruit. In other words, when we love the God-kind of way, we will not have a problem having joy. Knowing how to have patience while we're waiting for God to move in marriage shouldn't be hard when love is at the forefront. It is the love of God that helps us to show kindness even when mistreatment is involved. Love will allow us to operate in goodness, gentleness, faithfulness, and self-control. Again, it all springs forth from the root, which is love. Just like the branches are an extension of the vine, we can compare love to being the vine, while joy, patience, kindness, and gentleness can be considered the branches that grow out of the vine.

I Don't Feel Like It

When it comes down to operating in the fruit of the Spirit, you don't have to *feel like* loving in order to walk in love. And you will never *feel like* operating in longsuffering in order to obey God's commandment as you endeavor to try to suffer long. I am very blessed and grateful to God that He allows us to have feelings and emotions. God will have you know that feelings are not a prerequisite that must first be in place before we decide to walk in the God-kind of love. I'm praying that you catch that. Dr. Creflo Dollar said, "God gave us emotions, but they are not to govern our lives." I say this in all humility, but some of us need healing in our emotions.

God does not expect us to wait for a feeling before we decide to obey His commandment to love. Do you honestly believe Jesus *felt like* going to the cross to die? If He did, He would not have said in *Matthew 26:38, "My soul is deeply grieved, so that I am almost dying of sorrow."* (AMP) In verse 39, He says, *"My Father, if it is possible [that is, consistent with Your will], let this cup pass from Me; yet not as I will, but as You will."* (AMP) Does that sound anything like a statement from someone who was excited to go to the cross as an act of obedience? No, it does not. Jesus felt some way about dying on the cross. Jesus was one hundred percent man, and He was one hundred percent God. While in the garden of Gethsemane, the man side of Him wasn't thrilled about what He was about to experience on the cross. It was because He loved us so much that He carried out the will of the Father.

What gets us off track and in trouble in our marriages is there are far too many times that we sit around, waiting for a feeling before apologizing. Feelings are fleeting. They come and go. They are housed in the same emotions that will make you happy one minute and crying the next minute. Feelings and emotions are the reason that there is a thin line between love and hate. They are the culprit that is responsible for couples sleeping in separate bedrooms after a terrible argument or disagreement. Some married couples have made their way to divorce court because their feelings and emotions prevented them from humbling themselves under the mighty hand of God. Our feelings and emotions have started many arguments. Emotions have sent some of us into a fit of rage and have caused us to walk in pride and rebelliousness. Instead of putting our feelings in check to align them with the will of God, we have allowed our emotions to point us down a particular path. They have dictated to us which direction we should go in, how far we should go, how long we're allowed to stay there, and when to stop and make a u-turn so God can have His way in our lives. Our feelings and emotions have kept us from apologizing to our mates when God instructed us to do so, regardless of whether we were right or wrong. I know I parked in this area, but don't shoot me down when I'm speaking well because God wants us to take control of our actions by taking control of our feelings and our emotions.

If it can help someone, what I have found out on many occasions in my marriage is when I obeyed God, the feelings caught up some time later. Even if the feelings never catch up, there is always a blessing in obedience. If we wait for the sentiment first, we will never obey God. We are the ones who have been called by God and given the power of the Holy Spirit to point our emotions in the right direction. We are to be in control of our feelings because God calls us to set parameters around emotions. They are not supposed to be the boss of us. You can say amen to that. Let's follow in Jesus' footsteps and move out in obedience regardless of the price that has to be paid to obey God. Obedience will always cost you something, but are you willing to pay the price in order to receive the blessing?

The God-Kind of Love

If we want to keep from feeling like love is a second-hand emotion like Tina Turner, or if we're wondering what love's got to do with it, shouldn't we familiarize ourselves with how God commands us to love? Loving as God commands us to love is a big game-changer!

Let's go to *1 Corinthians 13:1–8*. It says, *"If I speak with tongues of men and of angels but have not love [for others growing out of God's love for me], then I have become only a noisy gong or a clanging cymbal [just an annoying distraction].And if I have the gift of prophecy [and speak a new message from God to the people], and understand all mysteries, and [possess] all knowledge; and if I have all [sufficient] faith so that I can remove mountains, but do not have love [reaching out to others], I am nothing. If I give all my possessions to feed the poor, and if I surrender my body to be burned, but do not have love, it does me no good at all. Love endures with patience and serenity, love is kind and thoughtful, and is not jealous or envious; love does not brag and is not proud or arrogant. It is not rude; it is not self-seeking, it is not provoked [nor overly sensitive and easily angered]; it does not take into account a wrong endured. It does not rejoice at injustice, but rejoices with the truth [when right and truth prevail]. Love bears all things [regardless of what comes], believes all things [looking for the best in each one], hopes all things [remaining steadfast during difficult times], endures all things [without weakening]. Love never fails [it never fades nor ends].* Let's drop down to verse *13: And now there remain: faith [abiding trust in God and His promises], hope [confident expectation of eternal salvation], love [unselfish love for others growing out of God's love for me], these three [the choicest graces]; but the greatest of these is love."* (AMP)

These verses say a lot concerning the God-kind of love. Please take time to read through them and meditate on them in your quiet time. As I previously stated, they are life-changing if we're willing to put them into practice. If I may, I would like to extract a few points from these verses. If the love of God is not fully displayed in your marriage, the Bible says we are nothing regardless of what we do or how much we give. Verse one says that even if we speak in tongues but don't have this kind of love, we have become nothing more than an annoying distraction. Wow! I most definitely don't want to be an annoying distraction in my marriage or otherwise. The scripture goes on to say that the God-kind of love endures all things. To endure in our marriage means that we are capable of holding out against every attack that comes against our marriage. It means to withstand every trick of the enemy while continuing to suffer patiently. It also means to go through and outlast while being persistent. It breaks my heart to say that I genuinely believe that this type of tenacity is missing in many marriages. Think about that for a moment.

How much do we, or are we willing to, endure the storm while patiently waiting for God? I am taking the time to walk through God's Word so we may learn how to stop throwing around the word "love" so loosely. I believe our marriage will go to another level and even another dimension as we put these scriptures into practice. God's Word will help us and show us what to do — *"When Out Isn't An Option."* Every action and every reaction should all spring forth from love. It is so easy for many people to give up and to give in before they begin applying God's Word to their circumstances. I'm talking about the God-kind of love here. It's imperative that I keep stressing that because I'm not talking about the feeling that gives you goosebumps when your spouse holds your hand or kisses you. That's all good in its place, but goosebumps don't keep a marriage intact — but the God-kind of love does. I'm praying that you have an ear to hear what the Spirit of God is saying.

The Bible says love is thoughtful and kind. It does not operate in jealousy or envy. Love is not rude or self-seeking. Love isn't overly sensitive or easily angered. I believe that we can sit and park right here. I know that plenty of women tend to be a bit overly sensitive. Being overly sensitive does not apply to all women. Nevertheless, I certainly believe that God made us to have a sensitive side to us. *Proverbs 25:24* says*, "It is better to live in a corner of the housetop [on the flat roof, exposed to the weather] Than in a house with a quarrelsome (contentious) woman."* (AMP) A contentious woman is a woman who is so controversial and so argumentative that she becomes too much to bear. I am sure that there are some men who are very quarrelsome as well, but there is a reason God pointed to the woman in that verse. It is not a good look on us, ladies.

Regardless of various situations that we experience in our marriage, it does not mean that God has given either spouse the green light to be easily angered or quarrelsome. An area many of us need to work on is being argumentative and quarrelsome. I'm talking about husbands and wives alike. It's terrible when spouses have to walk around on eggshells because we're not sure when our partner will blow up again. God expects us to have some self-control not only over our feelings and our emotions but also over our actions. Saying "God knows my heart" is not an excuse for having erratic and out-of-control behavior. *Proverbs 25:28 says, "Like a city that is broken down and without walls [leaving it unprotected] Is a man who has no self-control over his spirit [and sets himself up for trouble]."* (AMP)

A long time ago, cities had walls built around them to protect the people within the city. They probably still do. I'm not sure about that. They also had what they called "watchmen." The job of the watchmen would be to stand guard while looking for an enemy who would be approaching the city. The watchmen would warn the people of the approaching enemy. If the walls were down, the enemy could easily enter the city and attack its inhabitants. Proverbs 25:28 lets us know that when we have no self–control, we are like a city without walls. That is a recipe for disaster because it allows the enemy easy access to our lives. A lack of self-control, hatred, and contention is a portal that the adversary sees as an open invitation to come in and wreak havoc in our marriage. Don't allow a contentious and a quarrelsome spirit to get the advantage in your marriage. God tells us in *2 Corinthians 2:11* that *if we don't want the enemy to take advantage of us then we must not be ignorant of Satan's devices.*

The next verse that I would love to tackle is the one that says love doesn't take into account a wrong endured. God wants us to know that it's not His will for us to point fingers at each other constantly. I cover this in another chapter, but I would say this — at some point in marriage, the love of God in our hearts will help us greatly when we learn how to stop stirring the pot and allow things to simmer. Even when we have not made amends, there are times that we have to learn how to take off the boxing gloves and allow God to be God.

God tells us that love *bears* all things; it *believes* all things and *hopes* for all things. It remains steadfast during difficult times. It endures without weakening. My Lord! *Matthew 19:26 tells us that with men, many things are impossible.* I quoted this scripture in another chapter, but faith comes by hearing and by hearing the Word of God. I want you to know, dear heart, that with God, all things are possible if we only believe. God is the God of impossibilities. He can do all things but fail. Love never fades, nor does it ever fail. Now abides Faith, Hope, and Love, but the choicest and the greatest of these is love. That's what love has to do with it!

Tina Turner repeatedly says, "Who needs a heart when a heart can be broken?" As I stated earlier, I don't believe it's possible to stay married any length of time without having to endure a broken heart at some time or another during the marriage. I encourage those of us in the marriage that when we suffer a broken heart, let us give our brokenness to God. I know that you have heard it said, but God is the mender of broken hearts. When I read the Word of God, it lets me know that dealing with broken hearts is His specialty. It doesn't matter how many pieces your heart has been shattered into; God is the lifter-up of your head. If you can trust your heart to God, He is able to keep that which you commit to Him.

The Spirit of Offense

When hearts have been broken and shattered, the Bible warns us to be careful of the spirit of offense. What exactly is the spirit of offense? The spirit of offense is when someone we deeply love and care about has hurt and wounded us so badly, until it has become too difficult for us to let the offense go in order to receive proper healing. It's when we carry that pain around with us instead of seeking the face and the will of God concerning the assault. There are many times the offended carries the offense around for a lifetime. Unfortunately, some carry the offense to their graves. This spirit has broken up many marriages as well as many meaningful relationships. *Proverbs 18:19 says, "A brother offended is harder to win over than a fortified city, and contentions [separating families] are like the bars of a castle."* (AMP) This scripture lets us know how strong and damaging it is to harbor a spirit of offense. I can sense many who are reading this now are saying, "But you don't have a clue what they have done to me. You don't understand the depth of my pain or how I was crushed by their actions!" And you're right. I don't know, but God does.

We are treading on dangerous territory when we continue to carry around the spirit of offense. If we don't seek healing and offer forgiveness for the transgression, it causes us to walk around with bitterness. That bitterness begins to act like cancer in our bodies. In all reality, it is a cancer that has been embedded and deposited into our spirit man. And rest assured that this cancer that we have opened the door to, in turn, begins to affect our overall health. People have literally died from an illness because they were so angry and too bitter, they could not find a way to get over the pain and the heartache of the offense. We were not created or designed by God to carry around bitterness. The cancer of anger begins to spread, and before you know it, you will find yourself consumed with a stronghold you cannot overcome. A stronghold is just that. It is something that has such a tight grip on you; a chokehold that you cannot seem to get deliverance from, even when you have a strong desire to be delivered. The offense could have happened five, ten, fifteen, or twenty years ago, but that bitterness and spirit of offense will be alive and well, acting as if the offense happened only yesterday. That is a trick of the enemy people of God.

When we hold on to an offense, subconsciously, we are trying to make the person pay for their offense. We feel that if we forgive them and move on, they have somehow gotten away with the offense. *Romans 12:19 says,* *"Beloved, never avenge yourselves, but leave the way open for God's wrath [and His judicial righteousness],"* *for it is written (in Scripture),* *'VENGEANCE IS MINE, I WILL REPAY,' says the Lord."* (AMP) Who are we to try to make our spouses or other people pay for their offenses toward us? Have we become the Judge? The truth of the matter is some of us have become the Judge, the Jury, and the Prosecutor of our spouses. Some of us are guilty of wanting to see them pay. Deep down inside, some of us desire that they hurt just as badly as they have hurt us. We want them to pay while expecting God to let us off the hook when we offend Him with our disobedience. Say "AMEN," because it's the truth anyhow!

God is ready to touch you and heal you right in that spot you have kept covered up for so long. It's time for you to take off the bandage and receive some real healing from the hurt and pain you have carried for way too long. Healing is available to you. Give it to God. It's too much for you to carry around, and in addition to that, the pain has stolen your peace and joy. God sent His word to heal us. I genuinely want you to take this word to heart and hear the voice of God. Carrying around offense is a trick to keep you bound. We cannot praise, worship, or serve God to our fullest capacity when we are adamant about holding on to yesterday. When we learn how to operate in the God-kind of love, we can let go and offer forgiveness to the offender for the offense, thereby bringing liberation to our own lives that we can be healed for real!

When Forgiveness Seems So Undeserved

We forgive because God commanded us to forgive. *Mark 11:25–26* says, *"Whenever you stand praying, if you have anything against anyone, forgive him [drop the issue, let it go], so that your Father who is in heaven will also forgive you your transgressions and wrongdoing [against Him and others]. [But if you do not forgive, neither will Your Father in heaven for your transgressions]."* (AMP)

It's easy to feel as if forgiving our mates, as well as others, is so undeserving. I understand. I have felt that way many times in my marriage. We have not been called to determine whether forgiveness is deserved or not. God hasn't given us the authority to decide whether forgiveness is merited or unmerited. We have been called to obedience. As I previously stated, forgiveness is not about a feeling, but it's about a choice. The feeling has nothing to do with the choice we make to obey God. Once again, we make the mistake of tying our obedience to our emotions. Therefore, when we believe that our spouses have crossed the line and offended us, we sometimes think forgiving them lets them off the hook. I can assure you that forgiveness does not let them off the hook; instead, it lets us off the hook. When we forgive, it allows us to continue to have the liberty of having a relationship with God. Forgiveness allows us to keep receiving the refreshing that comes from the presence of God on a daily basis as we seek His face. It keeps the door open so we may continue to be blessed by God. When we refuse to forgive, I once heard that it's comparable to our drinking poison while expecting the offender to die. Being unforgiving is a blessing-blocker. And I don't know about you, but my relationship with God is too important to me to be intolerant toward anyone, especially my spouse. I don't want to experience standing on the outside of the presence of God, looking in and wondering why I cannot get a prayer through. I never want to wonder why I can no longer feel the presence of God in my prayer closet because I'm not willing to let go and let God. We must forgive! It's a commandment and not a choice. It is a commandment, and it's not to be treated and considered like a suggestion from God. At some point, we have to value our relationship with our heavenly Father so much that the relationship with Him is so fantastic and incredible, it trumps all other relationships. I have always been amazed by the truth that many people's horizontal relationships with others carry more weight and importance, and how it trumps the vertical relationship that they should have with God. The vertical relationship that we experience with God should be so important to us until it enhances all horizontal relationships across the board with people whom God has placed in our lives. We live out our relationship in our marriage based on how we live out our relationship with God. So, we should always be in the process of cultivating our walk with God.

The Crucifixion

Right before Jesus was crucified, *Luke 23:34* says, *"Father, forgive them; for they do not know what they are doing."* (AMP) What a powerful example of how God intends for us to handle offenses, wrongdoing, and betrayals. Nothing can demonstrate the love of God as much as the cross does. Jesus said, "Forgive them." If Jesus can forgive the very people who crucified Him, He expects us to follow in His footsteps. He forgave the same people that nailed Him to the cross. Can I ask how many of you have yet to be tied to a whipping post and beaten with a cat of nine tails until your flesh was ripped from your body? How many of you have been tied to a cross and had nails placed in your hands and feet with a thorny crown on your head? Love is more than a second-hand emotion. If you desire to stay married to the same person until death do you part, learn how to operate in the God-kind of love. It's God's way of keeping our marriages intact. I have purposed in my heart to always be in the process of working on my love-walk based on God's definition of love as opposed to my made-up version. God has called us to love. The Bible says in *John 3:16,* *"For God so loved the world"* that He sent Jesus to demonstrate and display the ultimate act of love. That, my friend, is the God-kind of love. I am convinced and fully persuaded that this type of love has everything to do with experiencing a happy, healthy, and loving marriage! We can give without loving, but we cannot love without giving of ourselves. Simply put, love has everything to do with it!

NOT EASILY BROKEN

Marriage is a calling. It is two people coming together, hoping to live out God's intended plan for a love relationship. Therefore, you don't just jump up and get married because you love the idea of being married. You don't get married because your best friend is married. I would dare to go as far as to say that you shouldn't just get married because you are in love. I already know that ruffled some feathers and somebody was taken aback by that statement, but it's true! Let me explain. Most people get married for the sake of love alone. I am one of them. I will admit that being in love is the best place to start when considering marriage, but it shouldn't be the only reason to "Tie the knot," as they say.

There are many unforeseen situations that will arise after a couple gets married. That's inevitable. But, many couples get married, and then down the road, they start trying to address things that should have been addressed before they said, "I do." It takes so much more than being in love. I am not saying a couple's marriage will not last if they get married for the sake of love alone. Here's my explanation of why two people should have more in common outside of love before getting married. The couple can be in love and not have the same goals or the same values, which can have severe repercussions five or ten years down the road. One can desire to start a family, while the other does not wish to have any children at all. You could be in love, but one of you could be a born-again believer, and the other isn't. There have been plenty of people whom I know and many I don't, who have had the assumption that once they married an unbeliever, they could change that person. They ended up learning the hard way that they cannot change ANYONE! It's extremely challenging for us to change ourselves, so why would we believe we can change others?

One day while driving to work, as I listened to a well-known pastor who was discussing the importance of having more things in common outside of love, before getting married, the teaching really blessed me. It was confirmation to what I am teaching here. He spoke about one couple who wanted to get marriage counseling sessions before their big day. As he sat across from the soon-to-be bride and groom, to his surprise, the lady was a born-again believer and the groom was not. He immediately began talking them out of getting married, but they insisted because they were madly in love. While I cannot remember if the pastor married them or not, the pastor said about a year later, the same couple who were so in love was in the process of getting a divorce. Unfortunately, they realized the love they shared wasn't sufficient enough to help them stay married. They loved each other, but they were unequally yoked.

For many of us who have been married for some time, we have soon come to realize that being in love alone cannot save a marriage. I know plenty of couples who were in love, got married, and, while still being in love, have also gotten a divorce. If love alone cannot save a marriage, love alone should not be the only factor in a couple's decision to get married. When it comes down to love, which should be the key ingredient in the marriage, many couples do not operate in the "God-kind of love." They don't live out their married lives based on loving the way that God's Word commands us to love. We will discuss that in another chapter.

In Ecclesiastes chapter 4, the writer speaks about many vanities and inequalities of life. *Ecclesiastes 4:9–12* says, *"Two are better than one; because they have a more satisfying return for their labor; for if either of them falls, the one will lift up his companion. But woe to him who is alone when he falls and does not have another to lift him up. Again, if two lie down together, then they keep warm; but how can one be one be warm alone? And though one can overpower him who is alone, two can resist him. A cord of three strands is not quickly broken."* (AMP)

First and foremost, in verse 9, where the scripture says two are better than one, this particular scripture isn't only speaking about married couples. The first few scriptures I previously stated tell us about "The power of two." I certainly believe that every David should have a Jonathan and every Mary should have an Elizabeth because two are better than one. But, for the sake of our topic, we will be speaking about the power of two concerning the marriage union.

While studying these scriptures, I was blessed when I read the John Gill concordance concerning Ecclesiastes 4:9, which states why two are better than one. It states, "They're better because they have a better reward or a better return for their labor." It says, "They have more of a pleasure and profit in each other's company and conversation." It furthermore states "It's better because as they serve one another in love, they also bear one another's burdens. They sharpen each other countenances, quicken and comfort each other's souls, establish one another in divine truth, and strengthen each other's hands and hearts." (John Gills Exposition of the Bible

Commentary (biblestudytools.com)   What a blessing! Who can deny that? These are some of the things that God intended for the marriage union. Yet another translation says "If one from the union falls, one can help the other up. Pity anyone who falls and has no one to help them up."

To further bless our hearts and describe God's intentions for the marriage union, Joseph Benson's concordance says, "If they fall in any way; into any mistakes, errors or sins, dangers, or distress, the one will lift up his fellow and hold him up." (https://www.studylight.org/commentaries/eng /rbc.html)

That blessed me because it lets us know, as part of the marriage calling, we have been called to lift one another up and not put one another down. We have not been called to count how often we have been wronged or ill-treated. Let's be honest here because we've all done it. I thank God that He does not count or hold my shortcomings against me before He decides to bless me or even approve of me. I am His beloved. In prayer, I often find myself saying to God that "I am the one He loves!" He loves me unconditionally, which means His love for me is not based upon my performance or lack thereof. We have to be careful of not trying to force our mates to perform before we accept and approve of them as a godly mate. If our acceptance is not based upon performance in the kingdom of God, why is our acceptance based upon performance when it comes down to marriage? Selah!

When you read Ecclesiastes 4:12, it says that *"And though one can overpower him who is alone, two can resist him. A cord of three strands is not quickly or easily broken."*(paraphrased) When the Bible says, "Though one can overpower him," the Bible is talking about an enemy, a thief, or a robber coming in to attack. In a marriage union, it's so important for us to fight against the spirit of division. One of the enemy's favorite modus operandi is to divide and conquer. The Bible lets us know that two can come together and resist the enemy by standing together, more than one can ever do alone. Two standing tall together in one accord, being of the same mind is greater than one of you fighting all by your lonesome. God would have you to know that standing together in one accord in prayer has a greater advantage against the enemy's wiles, than you can have individually, apart from your spouse. That's why the enemy cannot stand couples coming together in prayer. Have you ever noticed or wondered why the enemy fights the two of you so hard when it comes down to praying together? I believe God is telling us in this scripture that "We are better together."

In Ecclesiastes 4:12, when the Bible speaks of a strand of three cords, it's speaking about the man, the woman, and God as the third cord or the third strand. The bonds are much stronger when a couple includes God in their marriage union. The working of the Spirit of God in a three-fold cord marriage is to ensure that the marriage creates a stronger bond. The three-fold cords won't easily unravel. Therefore, the strong bond helps the couple to walk in greater unity, so the three strands have a better opportunity always to touch one another. When you take a rope and tie three strands together, you can best believe the three strands will always touch one another. A four or five-fold cord does not constantly touch each other as a three-fold cord does. A three-fold cord does not unravel as easily as long as they are all intact. It does not mean that the strands cannot separate, but it simply means that they are not easily broken. They are all intact, and they arc all touching each other. The threads are easily broken when you begin to untwist the individual cords. Therefore, a three-fold cord relationship requires the husband and wife to have some stick-to-itiveness with God as the head. The couple has to have the capability to continue to stand together even when it becomes difficult and unpleasant to keep standing. The question then becomes, "Can you stand to be blessed?" Can you stand until your desired change comes? Are you willing to pray and hold fast to the profession of your faith until something good happens and until a welcomed change shows up? I'm here to testify to you that this experience of waiting on

God and standing until can sometimes be a gut-wrenching experience. Waiting on the manifestation to show up will require all of God that's on the inside of you.

We all know that continuing to hope in God is something that a human isn't capable of, apart from the Spirit of God giving them some divine assistance. Please understand that I'm not talking about two couples who do not have a relationship with Christ that have decided to stay together in bitter, angry, and unhealthy marriages. I'm speaking of two people who are determined to have a marriage that God blesses. Keeping the strands tightly knitted together requires each couple to walk in more forgiveness than they are humanly willing to give. It takes God!

There was once a movie that my husband and I watched on Pure flix. I cannot remember the name of the film, but I could remember an elderly lady who wanted to desperately help in changing the lives of some young and talented but troubled teenagers. After she got involved, it wasn't long before she began thinking that she didn't have what it took to make a difference. These teenagers were very troubled in many ways. But, the elderly lady's heart was in the right place. It seemed as if the harder she tried, the more she seemed to be desperately failing in her quest to make a difference in their lives due to their level of anger and rebelliousness. Feeling like defeat was imminent and lurking at every turn, with every problem, she seriously began thinking about giving up on her dreams. But, before she did, she made an appointment to speak with one of the facility's owners, who happened to be her son, even though none of them knew it at that time. In the meeting, she asked the gentleman, "What do I do?" He responded by saying, "Just meet them where they are." She said, "And after that?" He replied to her, "Anything after that is a calling." That blessed me because when it seems like it's not working in our marriage, some of us want to give up and throw in the towel too soon. I know the frustration because just like you, we have been there many times. However, I believe we discredit the power and the ability of God. We eliminate "THE GOD FACTOR!" When you've gone as far as you can, as long as you can, that's when you will begin to notice and realize what I said earlier that marriage is a calling.

I know somebody can agree with me when I say you can go only so far in your own strength, might, wisdom and ability in marriage. You will soon come to discover that without God putting His super on your natural to help keep you strong and united, just like the lady in the movie, the strands will eventually begin to unravel — FAST! Just like in the film, we, too, must be willing to meet our spouses where they are if we're going to make a real difference.

Too often, it's difficult to stand and wait on God because in our sanctified minds, we believe where they are is too far beneath our standards. We begin thinking that where they are, is more than what we've bargained for, what we have signed up for, or what we can possibly stand. However, once we can come down from our high horses and begin meeting them where they are, the power of the Holy Spirit will start helping to propel us to get us to that next level.

Rocked to the Core

I remember when my husband and I had a severe challenge of meeting each other where we were. Just like you, we're still working on it every day. Because we were so challenged in meeting each other where we were, our marriage was rocked to the core. There was an open door, and the enemy gladly stepped through that door without haste. I could remember being so angry that I packed my suitcase and said to him, "I'm going by my sister's house for a few days in the morning!" The few times I felt compelled to leave, I always told him where I was going to keep the enemy from stepping in even more. So, I was all set to go the following day.

My husband was at work. When I woke up that day, I threw a few more things in my suitcase and was set to leave. Before I could make my way out of the front door, God used a good friend of mine to call me. She absolutely had no clue about what we were going through— so I thought. All I knew was I didn't share anything with her. When she called, the first thing she asked me was "What are you doing?" I said, "I'm about to leave. I'm going by my sister's house for a few days." Without me going into any further details, she said, "Thank you, Jesus. I'm so glad that I caught you before you left." She said, "The Lord told me to call you and to tell you not to leave the house, but to *stay and stand*." With tears running down my face, she continued to minister to me for forty-five minutes straight without me ever parting my lips to speak one word. While she was yet speaking, I felt myself fighting about whether I was going to obey God and allow God to have His way in this situation or if I was going to allow my anger, bitterness, and frustration cause me to walk in the flesh.

As this ordeal kept unfolding in my marriage, I kept trying to decide whether I going to disobey God due to my irritation, or was I going to obey God and allow Him to show Himself strong in my marriage again? While she was speaking, in between hearing what she was saying, I could remember all kinds of scriptures coming to my remembrance. I thought about *1 Samuel 15:22*, which says, *"Obedience is better than sacrifice."* (NLT) I thought about John 14:15 which says, *"If you [really] love Me, you will keep and obey My commandments."* (AMP) I desperately wanted to believe that I was sacrificing some things to the Lord for us to come back together again, but who was I fooling? I was mad as hell! But can I tell you that God expects us to obey Him at all costs, regardless of how we *feel about it?* God is looking for obedience. When our flesh, our feelings, and our emotions are in a standoff with the will of God, can I encourage you to go with God? When our feelings and emotions go in opposite directions, from being obedient to the will of God, we should always go with obedience and let the feelings catch up later.

So, after she finished ministering to me, I felt like I had a frog stuck in my throat. I was almost speechless. On the one hand, I was so blown away at the fact that God loves me so much that He would beat me to the punchline. On the other hand, I was also angry that God allowed her to catch me before I had an opportunity to get on the highway. God always has impeccable timing when it comes down to His divine will. Again, after ministering to me for forty-five minutes, she said, "Are you there?" I said, "Yes, I'm here and heard everything you said." I should have said that I heard everything God said because He used her mightily to get all up in my Kool-Aid! When I hung up the phone, I knew that I not only had to say "Yes" to her that I was still on the line, but I had to be willing to give God a "YES!" I had to let God know that I heard everything YOU said LORD!

What's more, I had to be willing to give God something to work with, so He could show Himself strong. And even though my flesh was screaming to let me know it *was not* in agreement with my final decision, I obeyed God. With my head hung down, I went into my bedroom and unpacked my clothes. As I was unpacking, I heard the Lord saying, "Unpack everything and put the suitcase back in the attic." He said, "I don't want there to be any evidence or even a trace of Shawn seeing that you were about to leave today." I'm still not sure of what all of that was about, but I trusted and obeyed God. I put all my underwear, bras, shirts, sweatpants, and shoes back in their proper places. And just as God said, when Shawn got home from work, he never had a clue that I was about to leave the house as I told him I would the night before.

For the strands to stay tightly knitted and in order to keep them from unraveling, we must be willing to obey God and step outside ourselves. Again, as God told Saul in *1 Samuel 15:22–23*, it says, *"To obey is better than sacrifice, and to heed [is better] than the fat of rams. For rebellion is as [serious as] the sin of divination (fortune-telling), And disobedience is as [serious as] false religion and idolatry."* (AMP)

We finally came back together and overcame that attack against our marriage, only for the enemy to rear his head again a few months later. I said, "God, You must have a serious blessing for us with our names on it to be picked out and to be picked on to this magnitude." And just like that, we were back at it again. I tell you, this time, it seemed like my head was spinning. It was as if it had come out of nowhere. We were right back into a three-week battle. I believe most of us do not know that there are times, just like in Job's case, when God and the enemy are making a pact over our lives. Sometimes, God asks Satan, "Have you considered my servant?" Now, thinking back on all that happened during this three-week trial, all I can say to this day is, "MY LORD!" If it had not been for the LORD on our side, we would not be together today. Yes, there had been many times that we argued and got into disagreements before, but there was something about this time that was so different and so scary. The previous trial I had discussed earlier was a cakewalk compared to what was going on with this trial. This time, our marriage was literally rocked to the core! The intensity of it had me thinking that the threads were sure to pop at any moment.

The cords had begun to unravel. Of course, I know I was still praying to God and reading His

Word. I also connected with a few others who prayed for us as it related to my marriage, while also encouraging me to stand. They prayed for God to restore what the enemy desperately tried to divide! I was touching God, and I believe my husband was just as prayerful. But, the unfortunate truth was Shawn and I were not touching each other spiritually or physically. There was no meeting of the minds.

Matthew 12:25 tells us that "Any kingdom that is divided against itself is being laid waste; and no city, or house divided against itself will [continue to] stand!" (AMP) Even though we both were touching God in our own ways individually, I believe that the separation, the anger, and division, coupled with the severity of the trial, kept us from touching God more profoundly than we needed to for our marriage to be restored. The two of us had totally lost the connection. And for the first time in many years, I had to fight against the thoughts that kept screaming to me that we might not make it through this one — this time!

Marriage should be for keeps, right? During this fiasco, I thought to myself so many times, should I go here or go there, or should I stay? This time, I actually had the clothes packed in the trunk of my car. And with clothes all ready to leave, I kept asking God the question, "What should I do, LORD?" I didn't want to operate in the flesh and be impulsive like I did on other occasions. I wholeheartedly sought the Lord before I made a move because I understood that my next move would be crucial. And just like a chess game, I understood that my next move could cause my marriage to come tumbling down. I kept sensing in my spirit not to leave! I began to notice my hair started falling out while I waited and tried my best to stand. I suffer from an auto-immune disease called alopecia. Therefore, in the midst of a trial, I struggle to maintain a full head of hair. I started losing weight because my heart was so heavy, and I felt so stricken with grief. I know that somebody is bearing witness with me.

We kept trying to meet each other at different times, hoping to reconcile, but to no avail. The times that we wanted to talk it out or to work it out, it turned into chaos and confusion all over again. Because we have a three-fold cord, though the strands began unraveling, the third strand, which is God Almighty Himself, kept the threads from ultimately coming apart. It is so vital to include God into the marriage union. He is truly the glue that holds a marriage together. After three weeks had passed, when we finally tightened up the three-fold cord again, and when all three of us began to touch all in unison, I still felt myself being apprehensive and fighting against the spirit of fear. The fight was because, even though I wanted to love hard again, I was apprehensive about letting go and letting God have His way. I kept thinking, "I never want my heart to ache like that again." When a person is hurting to a certain degree, they tend to put up a wall in hopes of protecting themselves. They began to operate in self-preservation. We don't have the power to keep or preserve ourselves. So, God gingerly began ministering to my heart, letting me know that He wanted to help to restore me again if I allowed Him to do so. I found myself being apprehensive to trust again. God said to me that He was not necessarily asking me to put my trust in my husband, but He wanted me to let go and put my trust in Him.

For a spell, I walked around with a sad countenance even after we made up. I kept on praying. I kept on studying God's Word. I even kept teaching Bible study every week, but the whole situation broke my heart. With a half-hearted smile on my face, I felt as if my heart was broken into so many pieces. My husband kept saying, "Adriene, I really want to see you smile again." I must say that he was really trying. I came to realize during this trial that we must have a willingness to become vulnerable in our marriage. Sometimes it's hard to allow our hearts to be vulnerable in the relationship, but we must continue to trust God with our marriage. When everything was said and done, the adversary thought he had left me for dead, but I got up. It's nothing wrong with being knocked down, but don't stay down. GET BACK UP AGAIN and get back into the fight! We were finally able to come back together again and began talking, laughing, and embracing one another simply because a three-fold cord is not easily broken. It cannot unravel easily when the couple includes God as the third strand!

For My Good

Another thing that will help us to keep the three stands tightly knitted together is when situations and challenges show up, we have to know that God is up to something good! He's a good, good God! We have to know that if God had never allowed trials to show up, they could not and would not show up. And when God does allow trials to show up, it's because He's trying to cause us to grow to another level. If we desire to succeed, we cannot spiritually stay in the same place in our marriages. God will allow some rain to fall. To grow and mature, we must be willing to lift and pick up on something heavy to flex those spiritual muscles of faith! And whatever He's allowing us to lift spiritually, it has to be heavier than what we're accustomed to carrying. It has to be something that will require God's help to help you carry. So, having said that, I believe one of the scriptures that is so difficult for Christians to grasp is *Romans 8:28,* which says, *"And we know [with great confidence] that God [who is deeply concerned about us] causes all things to work together [as a plan] for good for those who love God, to those who are called according to His plan and purpose."* (AMP)

Regardless of whether we just became born-again believers, saved for a short time or many years, it's complicated for many Christians to get this scripture from our heads into our hearts. Many of us have somehow convinced ourselves that when trials and tribulations make their way into our lives and marriage, there isn't any way for God to work it together "for the good." Let's make it personal. We sometimes *refuse* to believe that it's working together for the good of our marriage or in life, PERIOD! So, we subconsciously began this dialogue with God. "Well, God, is it just the things that I can understand with my human and finite mind that are working together for my good? Are you talking about those things, God?" And God says to us, "No — All things!" "Well, God, are things that work together for the good things that make me feel good and put a smile on my face, God?" God says, "No — All things!" "God, please tell me that you're not talking about the things that keep me up crying at night. Are you talking about those things, too, God?" God says, "All things, my daughter." "Well, God, I know that you're not talking about those things that tend to rip my heart apart and the things that leave me broken and my life shattered until I don't even know which way to turn next. Please tell me, Lord, that you're not talking about those things, right God?" God says, "All things, my son." The last time I checked, the Bible says to every born-again believer and to every believer who truly loves the Lord, "And we know that ALL THINGS are working together for our good." It's not just the things we perceive to be working together for our good. We must grasp that! The problem is that we don't know or fully understand that when God says all things, He literally means all things. He's speaking about the good, the bad, and the ugly.

One thing I absolutely love about God is that God does not send everything, but He uses everything to help us to grow up in Him. When the unthinkable shows up, my prayer for you is that you would say, "It's for my good. I don't like it, but it's working together for my good. I wished I didn't have to be bothered with it, but it's all working together for my good because God said it would!"

Can We Just Agree

Regardless of how much couples *try* to get along and *try* to be in one accord, it's impossible to be in one accord void of the power of agreement. What has always baffled me is how couples keep trying to walk together and be in one accord without being in agreement with one another.

1 Corinthians 1:10 says, "Now I beseech you, brethren, by the name of our Lord Jesus Christ, that ye all speak the same thing, and that there be no divisions among you; but that ye be perfectly joined together in the same mind and in the same judgment." (KJV) Be quick to agree with one another by allowing God's Word to be the final authority. There is power in agreement. I know firsthand that there will be times when we, as a couple, are not as quick to agree. It's something that I am genuinely working on in my marriage.

God desires to bless us tremendously in our marriage. We have to have a made-up mind that we must commit to working at our marriage continuously because we never arrive. I can promise you that when all three stands continue to touch, you and I can rest assured that God will see to it that our union will be a marriage that is "Not Easily Broken," because two are better than one!

KNEELING IN ORDER TO STAND

As we awake to see the start of a brand-new day, every morning, I believe there are so many things that are pulling at us. Everybody wants some of our time or is in need of some of our attention. There are appointments to be kept and deadlines we must meet. We begin to wonder if we will ever return that important phone call while considering what we're going to eat or cook for dinner.

For many of us, life can seem to be a never-ending hustle. If the truth was to be told, it can become very draining and taxing if we never learn how to prioritize our schedules. God wants life to be enjoyed and not just endured. We must have a prayer life to endure and stay the course. We must be able to kneel in order that we can stand against the wiles of the enemy. For those who cannot kneel, God is more concerned about the attitude and posture of our hearts rather than if our knees can still physically support us in prayer. God has a vested interest in you and is looking for you to posture your heart before Him in worship and continuously seek His face. In other words, I'm talking about having an intimate relationship with our heavenly Father continually. Occasionally, I have heard people say they need more time to pray. My answer to that statement would be that we must *make time* because we cannot afford not to pray.

Out of every chapter I have written in this book, this chapter about prayer is most dear to my heart. The reason is because I don't know where I would be if I had never cultivated a genuine and intimate prayer life in my walk with God. I am convinced of this one truth — that if my husband and I had started our married lives void of prayer, we probably would not be married today. Even today, if we don't maintain a consistent life of prayer, and constant intimacy with our heavenly Father, what miserable lives we would be living. I could not imagine having a healthy marriage outside of prayer. I'm not saying that we don't have our fair share of challenges because we all do. We're just like any other couple regarding challenges, but prayer has been an enormous asset in our lives. There was once a time in my life when I did not take prayer as seriously as I do today. I will admit that. None of us start this Christian journey as spiritual giants in the realm of prayer. At least, I don't believe we do. I lacked a prayer life for many years after becoming a born-again believer. It was because I was either spiritually immature or didn't know any better. Even though I had a prayer life, it wasn't much to write home about, as they say. Even though I prayed, I didn't understand the importance and the value of a prayer life as I do today. My Lord, I thank God for growth!

I hope you know, my friend, that prayer should be a lifestyle for every born-again believer. I am not here to condemn anyone because we all are growing. It's no secret that there are many Christians who do not pray on a consistent basis. Prayer is not an option, but it must be considered a necessity. It should not be a choice that we somehow get to choose to do when it's convenient for us or something that we do out of desperation or as a last-ditch effort to see the hand of God move on our behalf. We must be aware of the fact that prayer is something God has commanded us to do. That's right. God commanded us to pray! *Matthew 6:5* starts by saying, *"Also, when you pray."* It does not say *"If you pray."* We do ourselves a great injustice when our lives lack consistent times of daily-ongoing prayer. We should be grateful that God allows us to pray and partner with Him in carrying out His will in the earthly realm. As we grow in our faith and relationship with the Father, we begin to get rid of the mindset that we *have to pray* and began thanking God for the opportunity He gives us to come into His presence to pray. What a privilege and an honor that has been made available to us. As we grow in God, we start taking on the mindset that God loves us so much that we *get to pray.*

Prayer is how we invite God to intervene in our lives. Prayer is the believer's authority to speak into the atmosphere, then step back and watch the hand of God move in our various situations as well as in the lives of so many others who we are interceding and seeking God's will. Prayer gives us the opportunity to touch the nations in places all over the world that we will never physically be able to visit in person. Prayer is our way of conducting spiritual warfare against the forces of darkness. It's a way that God has allowed us to make heavenly interruptions that will take precedence over the works, schemes, and tricks of the enemy. *John 10:10 says, "The thief comes only in order to steal and kill and destroy. I came that they may have life and abundance [to the full, till it overflows]."* (AMP) Jesus is warning us of the enemy's plan for our lives. Through prayer, He also gives us the authority to intercept those things the enemy is trying to do. You can best believe that the forces of darkness are constantly at work trying to destroy you, your marriage, your children, and everything that concerns you. I am so thankful to God that He's given us such a powerful weapon in prayer!

One of the things I love the most about prayer is that it helps me to draw closer to my heavenly Father. It allows me to have a dynamic relationship with God that I would otherwise forfeit. Prayer gives me the confidence I need to know that regardless of what happens in life, God promises never to leave or forsake me. Because I touch God in prayer, it gives me the confident assurance I need that allows me to know I don't *have to* choose to walk in the spirit of fear. The Bible tells us in *1 John 4:18 that "Perfect love casts out fear."* The NIV version says *"Perfect love drives out fear."* That alone should encourage us to get into that secret place with God because fear is in full operation in these last and evil days. We need something to drive fear from our midst, and prayer is just the tool God gives us to dispel the spirit of fear. I can truly testify that the closeness I experience with God through prayer is priceless! And that's the same relationship God desires to share with all His children. He sent Jesus to die on the cross to afford us the opportunity to commune with Him through the power of prayer. Think about that. Jesus died not only that we could be saved, delivered, and set free, but God was looking to cultivate a relationship so He could start a dialogue with His people!

No Weapon

Prayer is such a powerful weapon! So, now that we know what the enemy's modus operandi is based upon, *John 10:10,* let's talk about the victory God has given us to combat the enemy's plans. *Isaiah 54:17 says, "'No weapon that is formed against you will succeed; And every tongue that rises against you in judgment you will condemn. This [peace, righteousness, security, and triumph over opposition] is the heritage of the servants of the LORD, And this is their vindication from Me,' says the LORD."* We can take comfort in knowing that God tells us that no weapon the enemy has formed against us will succeed or prosper. We learn here that God never promised us the weapons would not form. Weapons from the enemy are constantly being formed against us for our demise — especially in marriage. The enemy hates godly marriages.

The promise spoken here in Isaiah 54 was not only for the future of the Israelites, but it still applies to the church today. Even though the enemy will form weapons, God gives us the weapon of prayer to overcome every weapon the enemy has developed and will form. If you would read the previous verses in Isaiah 54, God says to us that He is the one who created the blacksmith. He's the one who is over the one who made the weapons. God created the enemy and the destroyer who comes up against us in hopes of destroying us and wreaking havoc in our lives. And because He was the one who created the enemy, He is also the one who decides that those weapons will be ineffective against our marriage and in every other area of our lives. In other words, God is the one who is in charge. The enemy does not get to choose whether the weapons will succeed. You need to know this. I know I'm laboring this point, but I sense in the spirit that many of you need to know this truth. It's so essential for you to know that when it comes down to marriage, God is the one who makes the final decision to say to the enemy,

"Stop, that's enough!" We do not have to allow the enemy to destroy our marriage. He didn't orchestrate it and he does not have the authority to destroy what God has joined together, unless we give him that authority. God can draw a line in the sand and tell the enemy not to cross certain lines, just as He did in the life of Job. I know many times, it seems as if the weapons are getting an advantage, but my friend, God has the final say on the prospering of every weapon that has been formed and launched against us.

Isaiah 54:17 says this is the peace and security that belong to the righteous. He says that this is our vindication from Him. I'm not sure how many of you read the Message Bible, but *Isaiah 54:17* in the Message Bible ends the chapter by saying, *"'Any accuser who takes you to court will be dismissed as a liar. This is what God's servants can expect. I'll see to it that everything works out for the best.' God's Decree"* My Lord, I don't know about you, but I'm shouting hallelujah right about now! God promised us that regardless of what happens or what shows us, we have the assurance that He will see to it that everything works out for the best because the enemy will always be found to be a liar in the throne room of heaven! Glory to God! This promise from God is the portion that has been allotted to us by God. You and I are co-laborers with God. I'm speaking to born-again believers here. And because we are co-laborers with God, we cannot expect God to make sure that everything works out for the best in our lives if we refuse to do what He has commanded us to do — and that is to pray. A lack of prayer gives the enemy an open door to prosper and succeed in his attacks against us. Again, God has put at our disposal the power of prayer.

Effectual Fervent Prayers

James 5:16 says "The effectual fervent prayer of a righteous man availeth much." (KJV) What an awesome promise that God has given us. The Word of God tells us what is available to a righteous man who prays. This promise isn't for any and everyone. For those of us who are not perfect, but are walking upright before God, we have been given permission by God to offer up effectual fervent prayers. An effectual fervent prayer is a prayer that is active and passionate. It's a prayer that is energetic and heartfelt. God doesn't expect the believer to come before Him with a lukewarm and lifeless prayer hoping to receive something. He doesn't expect us to drag ourselves before Him with a prayer that does not mean anything to us, but we're just offering up meaningless, random words hoping that something would stick. God tells us to come boldly before Him. He wants us to come full of the assurance that He is not only a God who hears our prayers, but also a prayer-answering God. He does not sleep, and neither does He slumber. So, effectual fervent prayers are prayers that are active and effective. God desires for us to pray without ceasing because effectual fervent prayers prevail. And because efficacious prayers avail much, they get results. Because this type of prayer is productive in the Spirit realm, it can disarm the works of the wicked. Therefore, when you get up off your knees or however you posture yourself before the Lord, even though your situation might look the same, you can take heart that something has changed in the Spirit realm. I'm not talking about continuous cycles of two-minute prayers. I'm talking about when you go down on your knees and you are passionate about what you're seeking God for as you pray and petition God. I'm talking about when the sincerity of your heart is able to touch the heart of God. So much so that when you are finished praying, you will notice that God has given you another perspective on how you view your situation. This new perspective will change the way you look at what you're looking at! Did you catch that? Listen, people of God, it's hard to stand when you haven't quite learned how to kneel before the Lord in prayer.

The Bible tells us in *Ephesians 6:13–14*, *"After we have done all to stand, stand therefore."* (paraphrased) The Message Bible says, *"Be prepared. You're up against far more than you can handle on your own. Take all the help you can get, every weapon God has issued, so that when it's all over but the shouting, you'll still be on your feet."* Hallelujah! Talking about kneeling in order to stand! My point here is when you have given it your best and once you have learned how to kneel in prayer before the Lord, that's when you will be able to stand! You have yet to do all until you have learned how to get into the presence of the LORD! Some of you are trying your very best to stand, but the problem with you trying to stand is that you have yet to kneel on an everyday basis. Get into God's presence and keep on asking. Get into His presence and give Him no rest concerning His promises!

Persistent Faith

Jesus was always in the practice of teaching His Disciples. He always spoke parables to them. In Luke 18, we will find one of the parables that Jesus was speaking to the Disciples. He was letting them know the importance of a consistent prayer life as well as the importance of having consistent faith in Him. In *Luke 18:1–8, it says, "Now Jesus was telling the disciples a parable to make the point that at all times, they ought to pray and not give up and lose heart, saying, 'In a certain city, there was a judge who did not fear God and had no respect for man. There was a [desperate] widow in that city, and she kept coming to him and saying, "Give me just and legal protection from my adversary." For a time, he would not, but later he said to himself, "even though I do not fear God nor respect man, yet because this widow continues to bother me, I will give her justice and legal protection; otherwise by continually coming she [will be an intolerable annoyance and she] will wear me out."' Then the Lord said, 'Listen to what the unjust judge says! And will not [our just] God defend and avenge His elect [His chosen one] who cry out to Him day and night? Will He delay [in providing justice] on their behalf? I tell you that He will defend and avenge them quickly. However, when the Son of Man comes, will He find [this type of persistent] faith on the earth?'"*

As we stand our ground, we can rest assured that the enemy is our adversary. And as a child of God, it is our God-given right to go before the Lord consistently. Jesus was letting the disciples know that if this unjust judge, who did not fear God, was willing to answer a prayer request from this widow, who was persistent in her coming, how much more will our heavenly Father answer the prayers of those of us who don't give up in asking. If a desperate widow could move the hand of a man who did not revere God, how much more can we, who have been bought with a price, move the hand of a loving Father? We have to have persistent faith. We have to have a level of desperation. I know it often feels so easy to give up on praying for our mates and marriage. It sometimes feels like such a daunting task weighing you down, but God tells us to keep coming to Him in prayer. Don't get weary in well-doing. Continue to put God in remembrance of His Word that He has spoken concerning your marriage. It's a test of our faith. Our marriages are most definitely worth fighting for, so make sure that you pass the test!

The Three Realms of Prayer

I want you to know that one of my main goals and desires in ministering about prayer as we trust God for our marriage and every situation that challenges our faith, is to move us from the outer courts to the inner courts. In *Matthew 7:7–8*, the Bible says, *"Ask and keep on asking and it will be given you; seek and keep on seeking and you will find; knock and keep on knocking and the door will be opened to you. For everyone who keeps on asking receives, and he who keeps on seeking finds, and to him who keeps on knocking, it will be opened."* (AMP) The element of asking, seeking, and knocking are all realms of prayer that one can reach. As I share with you the three realms of prayer, I want you to know that this is not an ABC action plan to learn how to touch the heart of God. I realize and understand that all born-again believers have their own personal relationship with God, and the way that God moves in one of our lives doesn't necessarily means that's the way He moves in the next person's life. Therefore, as I explain the different realms of prayer, your experience with God might be quite different because we all are in different places in our walk with God.

I once taught this at a conference, and it really blessed the lives of the people of God. I was led to share it again, simply because I don't want the child of God to become frustrated in their prayer life because they feel as though they are not getting results as they attempt to seek God in prayer.

The Asking Realm

When Jesus tells us to ask, asking is the first realm of prayer. And because asking is the first realm of prayer, when we begin asking, we are in the outer courts. As we come before the Lord in prayer, we start off in the asking realm. There is absolutely nothing wrong with asking God for the things we need. *Philippians 4:6 says, "Do not be anxious or worried about anything, but in everything [every circumstance and situation] by prayer and petition with thanksgiving, continue to make your [specific] requests known to God."* (AMP) God does not have a problem with us asking. As I previously stated, God encouraged the Disciples in *Luke 18:1* to keep asking. He told them to be persistent in prayer. My point here is that, even though God doesn't have a problem with us asking, don't stop in the asking realm. The asking realm should not be the place where we end our prayers to go and start the day. Too many times, some believers get so caught up in asking and asking, crying and asking, that they stay in a perpetual state of asking God to move by His Spirit, without moving further into prayer. Unfortunately, many Christians never move past the state of asking. Furthermore, if they don't see the hand of God move, they get back on their knees at a later date and time, only to begin the process of asking all over again before walking still feeling sad and disappointed. We need to understand that as a believer, after we have let our requests be made known unto God, He wants and desires for us to move from that place of asking in the outer courts to begin seeking His face in the inner courts. Asking, for so many, is nothing more or less than a desperate plea to see the hand of God move. When we are only interested in seeking God's hand, we are not genuinely seeking His face. If we learn to seek His face, His hand will automatically move in our lives.

As I previously stated, many Christians hang out in the asking realm most of their lives. In this first realm of prayer, too many have thrown in the towel because they believe that God didn't move the way they thought He should have moved. Therefore, they stay down and out while continuing to carry the weight of the world on their shoulder. As a result, they remain in a state of depression because they don't realize that God has so much more that awaits them if they would only learn how to tarry in His presence. In order to move beyond this first realm of prayer, we must have the wherewithal to dwell in God's presence without feeling rushed to go and take on our day. Abiding in the presence of God requires us to put our flesh under subjection. We must bind up the spirit of anxiety and ask the Holy Spirit to quiet our thoughts in the presence of God. It is very important to learn how to still ourselves in God's presence while in the outer courts, because in the outer courts, most times, we are still operating in the flesh. In this realm of prayer, our thoughts can be in a thousand different places. One way that God has given me to still my thoughts is to listen to soaking music as I begin to meditate on the Word of God. I begin thinking about the goodness of the Lord as I open my mouth and begin to give God the praise that is due His name. God wants us to know that when we pray, we must believe that He hears us. And if we know that He hears us, we know that we have the petitions that we desire of Him.

The Seeking Realm

The seeking realm is the second realm of prayer. Again, it's called "The inner courts." In this innermost place, the Spirit of God will begin to dry our tears that stem from worry, depression, and anxiety. In this place of intimacy with the Lord, we start to believe His word much more than we did when we were in the outer courts. The chains and strongholds of fear began falling off of us as we start to experience the peace of God that surpasses all understanding. In the inner courts, we began to have the confident assurance to believe the Word of the Lord found in *Numbers 23:19,* which says, *"God is not a man, that He should lie, Nor a son of man, that He should repent. Has He said, and will He not do it? Or has He spoken, and will He not make it good and fulfill it?"* (AMP)

The inner court is the place where we began confessing "If God said it, I believe it, and that settles it." And even though your situation hadn't changed in the natural, you begin to sense that something has changed and taken place in the realm of the Spirit. God begins to give you a different perspective that you did not have when you were hanging out in the asking realm. When we get into the inner courts, that's the place where we really start to believe that God is going to "Make it good!" Most times, when I'm in the inner courts, tears begin to run down my face. I begin feeling the presence of the Holy Spirit more than I did in the outer courts. As I persist in prayer, I begin hearing the voice of God comforting me while letting me know "It is well," regardless of my present circumstances.

While in the outer courts, I have learned that I was the one who was having more of a monologue with God. God allowed me to pour out my heart to Him. In the inner courts, the Spirit of God has joined in the conversation, and at this point, there is a dialogue taking place. In this place, God is now pouring out His Spirit upon me. In the inner courts, while I am basking in the presence of the Lord, I no longer feel as desperate about my situation and my tears are no longer tears of sorrow, but they are now tears of joy. I can go on and on about the inner courts. But, I leave you with this. I believe the reason we begin to experience peace and joy in the inner courts is that Psalms 16:11 says, *"You will show me the path of life; In Your presence is fullness of joy; In Your right hand there are pleasures forevermore."* (AMP) It's hard to get into the presence of God and not experience the joy of the Lord. Glory to God!

The Knocking Realm

And, of course, the knocking realm is the third realm of prayer we get to visit supernaturally. This realm brings us right into the Holy of Holies, which is the very throne room of God. In this realm, God is having His way. When you enter into this realm of prayer, you will find yourself in total awe at the glory of God! While in the Holy of Holies, which is the knocking realm, you're not concerned about what time it is or what's on the agenda for the day. It's all about God's Shekinah glory! Many believers don't experience this realm of prayer in their own prayer closets in the privacy of their homes. I believe it's because in order to get to this third realm of prayer, first and foremost, time must not matter any longer. When Moses went up to the top of Mount Sinai, the Bible tells us that he was there for forty days. He didn't have anything to eat, nor did he have anything to drink. God was his sustenance. How many of us are willing to make that kind of sacrifice?

Another reason many believers don't enter into the knocking realm of prayer is that we're not willing to crucify the deeds of the flesh. In order for the Spirit of God to usher you into the Holy of Holies, you must be willing to crucify your flesh because flesh cannot enter into the very presence of God. If you will read Isaiah 6:1, it says, *"In the year that King Uzziah died, I saw also the Lord sitting upon a throne, high and lifted up, and His train filled the temple."* (KJ21) The Prophet Isaiah was speaking in these scriptures. He goes on to talk about how the Angels cried out by saying, *"Holy, holy, holy,"* as they worshipped God. Isaiah 6:4 says, *"And the posts of the door moved at the voice of him that cried, and the house was filled with smoke. Then said I, 'Woe is me, for I am undone, because I am a man of unclean lips and I dwell in the midst of a people of unclean lips; for mine eyes have seen the King, the LORD of hosts."* (KJ21)

As we read these scriptures, I am comfortable in saying that the Prophet Isaiah was not in the outer courts when he was having this experience. He had moved beyond the inner courts. The Prophet was in the Holy of Holies. It is only when you enter into the Holy of Holies that God will allow you to see yourself to this magnitude. In the Holy of Holies, sometimes all you can do is weep before the LORD as you experience His glory in ways that others do not experience, when they are not willing to abide in the presence of the Lord. The Prophet Isaiah said *"Woe is me, for I am undone."* The presence of the LORD allowed him to see himself in a way that he probably never saw himself before this mind-blowing experience. As you read, you'll see how conviction fell upon the Prophet as he stood before the LORD. Can I tell you that he was not in the outer courts asking the LORD of LORDS for anything at this point? In this realm, it becomes all about God and not about what you have need of because you have passed the asking realm.

I also would like to say that we do not move from one realm of prayer to the next realm of prayer just because we have a desire to do so. It's only when we learn how to wait on the Lord in our secret place that the Spirit of God will usher us into that next realm of prayer. There is no certain time limit that we can set on our watch as to when God will allow us to visit the next realm of prayer. But, as you stay in that place of intimacy with

God, just like we open the door to let someone into our homes, the Spirit of God will open the door and invite you to go deeper.

While I do not intend to do an in-depth study on the three realms of prayer, I want to encourage you to learn how to wait on God in prayer. There is more to prayer than asking God for the things that we have need of in our lives. Prayer must be more than a plea of desperation. We must learn how to carve out some quality time in our schedules so we can get alone with God.

Prayer— Boring or a Blessing

I have literally had a conversation with a person or two who has expressed to me that they believed prayer was boring. I'm sure they are not alone. If you are someone who believes that prayer is boring, I certainly understand why you don't engage in it as much as you should. I once felt that way. I can shed some light and give encouragement to those who believe prayer is boring. Listen, I don't know everything that there is to know about prayer. But, what I have realized that when I pressed past the outer courts, and into the inner courts, that's when prayer became more enjoyable to me. I had to press past my flesh before I began enjoying fellowship with God. As I waited for God while worshipping God, I could sense when the Spirit of God was inviting me to move further into the presence of God. As I moved further into His presence, I realized that I was no longer heavy of heart. I realized that as I began to think about the goodness of the Lord, a genuine praise and worship began to overshadow my sadness. I began feeling the Spirit of God more, as opposed to wondering what I had to do in the next hour. When a person learns how to consistently schedule time to be with the Lord, they will also begin to recognize how the Spirit of God will start to beckon them to spend more time in God's presence. You will begin to long to be in His presence more than a person who is in the desert longs to get a drink of water.

There is something so special about prayer that when you understand that you are actually in communion with the KING of KINGS and the LORD of LORDS, you will no longer consider prayer to be boring. It becomes a mind-blowing, life-altering experience. As I previously stated, you begin to become addicted to the very presence of God as He starts beckoning for you more and more to come and spend some quality time with Him. We cannot afford to have lives void of consistent prayer.

I want to revisit *James 5:16, which says, "The heartfelt and persistent prayer of a right man (believer) is able to accomplish much [when put into action and made effective by God — it is dynamic and can have tremendous power]."* Somebody say amen to that! When we as believers, go into consistent, daily, and ongoing prayer that is heartfelt, it can accomplish much. This scripture tells us it is dynamic and can have tremendous power. Who wouldn't want to achieve those kinds of results? It has to be heartfelt. I can tell you that if it really doesn't mean anything to you, it really doesn't mean anything to God. God does know our hearts. We cannot be lazy when it comes down to prayer, Saints of God.

I am sharing with you my experiences in prayer because there are levels, realms, and dimensions of prayer that many of us have yet to tap into as we continue to grow in God. There is more awaiting us. I have yet to arrive when it comes down to my prayer life. I too, have a stronger desire to go deeper in prayer. Nevertheless, God has shown me how to elevate in prayer from one level to another level and from one dimension to the next dimension.

I have noticed that there have been times when I come away from the asking realm in the outer courts, bogged down and wondering about all of the things I have to do and whom I need to call back, that I was able to trust God in prayer more in the areas where I was seeking God. When I'm not rushing God with my ten minutes of prayer, I have been able to move into the inner courts. I have been to a place in worship where all I could do was sit there in the presence of God, crying and weeping in awe at His glory. And when the enemy has tried to bring depression upon me from marriage challenges to anything else, moving from the asking realm has helped lift depression off me. It has helped me stand and trust God when I didn't know what else to do.

Prayer has acted like a relief valve in my life. A relief valve, also known as a pressure relief valve, is a device that lowers the pressure to prevent damage to a system. Its function is to protect pressure-sensitive equipment from damage caused by overpressure. Again, they are critical in a pressure system to avoid explosion, loss of equipment, as well as injury. My God, what a revelation! One of God's plans for our prayer life is to prevent us from having a system failure in our hearts and minds. Prayer and worship will open up the heart as the Spirit of God begins to release much of life's build-ups that we experience on a daily basis. God knows that life can be very fragile. Most of us have heard the saying "Pressure bust pipes!" And all I'm trying to convey is that prayer can and will relieve some of life's pressure in our lives. That is what the power of prayer will do in our lives. I pray that you will learn how to pray without ceasing.

We have to know that these types of results will cost us something. God is longing for a more intimate relationship with you through prayer! Prayer is a powerful weapon. Are you willing to pay the price? Are you ready to "Kneel in order that you may be able to stand?" I am rooting for you!

THE SUFFICIENCY OF GRACE

I have so much to be proud of in all my years of living. I have accomplished many noteworthy things. I've reached some significant milestones that can only be accredited to the goodness of God in my life. Even though I have done many things right, I've also gotten many things wrong. I have made so many mistakes and have had so many mishaps on my Christian journey. I have often stopped at certain junctures in my life and wondered why God even put up with me. Have you ever felt that way? In these thirty-one years of holy matrimony, many unholy decisions have been made on both our parts. I had done things God told me not to do when I knew better. I had followed my heart's desire when that desire caused me to lose my connection with God, which is of great value to me. There have been times when I took my sweet time to forgive my husband when the Spirit of the Lord prompted me to forgive. Can I tell you that delayed obedience is still disobedience? If you haven't found yourself in any of these scenarios, sit tight because I am heading your way.

I can testify to the truth that there have been times when I knew God was telling me to hold my tongue to avoid chaos, conflict, and confusion. Sometimes, I have decided I wanted to operate in the flesh only to suffer the consequences on the back end. How many of you know that our adversary will never show you the end of a thing? He will never show you the end result of operating in rebellion and disobedience against God. However, he will show you the beginning of a thing. He'll always dangle something before us just enough to try to tempt us to go *all in*. See, he knows that if we saw the end of our rebellious actions or the consequences we'd have to face, we would walk away to avoid a lot of pain and heartache in our marriage. Am I right about it? I said all of that to say that I don't know where I would be today if it had not been for God's love and grace in my life and on my side. God extends to us all so much grace and mercy.

See, mercy and compassion from God is when He holds back from us that which we *do deserve,* and grace is when He gives us that which we *don't deserve.*

The grace of God can be defined as the unmerited favor and the divine assistance that God gives to us. When something is unmerited, that means we cannot work for it. We cannot pay for it, and we cannot earn it. Not only is grace the unmerited favor of God, but it's also the loving-kindness of God, the warm-heartedness, tender-heartedness, and big-heartedness of God. Grace is God's helpfulness, caring, thoughtfulness, consideration, and sympathetic nature. His love and compassion toward us are expressed through the grace that He so freely gives us. I once read something that blessed me concerning the grace of God. It said, "God's grace fills in the holes of life that other things we try to rely on cannot." My Lord, what a mighty God we serve.

Every marriage relationship needs grace and mercy if it is going to survive. I'm talking about unconditional love and kindness toward one another. In marriage, we need the kind of mindset that says freely we receive God's grace and freely should we extend grace to our spouse. How can we receive God's grace, yet not be willing to turn around and extend that same grace we have received? In our marital relationship, our spouse should not have to try to work for or to earn the grace that should be extended to them when they miss the mark. We must remember that we too, miss the mark plenty of times. We too, fall short of the glory of God. When there is trouble in paradise, even if we believe we are on the receiving end, God still expects us to show love and compassion through grace without any strings attached. In other words, it must be freely given without being based upon the right conditions being met first. We must extend grace whether we believe they are deserving of it or not. Trust me, I have been there before. I had held back from extending God's grace to my husband when I was angry because there were times when I felt like he didn't deserve it — PERIOD! Come on here. I am talking the real talk here! Because I'm being transparent, I have to admit that I was wrong in my way of thinking. That way of thinking is not biblical, but it is selfish and fleshly. How can we call ourselves waiting for the right conditions to offer grace when we do not deserve God's loving kindness and tender mercies that He shows us daily? Can I tell you that God is more interested in the two of you being *reconciled,* than He is in who's *right* versus who's wrong? God is the God of reconciliation.

He's a God of restoration. I had significantly experienced suffering in our marriage, even when I was right based upon the Word of God. You ought to stop and think about that for a moment! How many times have you found your marriage suffering even when you were right? Who cares! Sometimes, we believe God should give us brownie points when we're right. God is not interested in providing us brownie points when we're still very much divided. It doesn't matter who's right when the enemy is having his way. We must be willing to lose as an individual, so we can win as a couple who is so deserving of God's best. If one of you is losing, then both of you are still losing in the realm of the Spirit. You are one! So, there is no need to rejoice there or to take a victory lap! Because marriage has made us one in spirit, we both might as well win over the forces of darkness. And likewise, if one of you wins, you both win. You might as well win together as a couple. The Bible says in *2 Corinthians 1:4 that God is the one "who comforts and encourages us in every trouble so that we will be able to comfort and encourage those who are in any kind of trouble, with the comfort with which we ourselves are comforted by God."* (AMP)

I genuinely believe that marriage has so many incredible benefits that we can enjoy. I pray that you often enjoy beautiful times of peacefulness and joy in your marriage, as do my husband and I. I pray that you will always keep the playfulness in your midst and times of laughter in your marriage. Never stop saying "I love you" or giving one another a kiss as you pass by each other in the house. All of these things keep the sparks burning and make for a more healthy and happy marriage. But, we cannot take the good and not be willing to deal with the sometimes troubling things in our marriage. Sometimes, the enemy will come along and try to torment us. God gives us His grace to deal with those things that are tremendous sources of aggravation and frustration. Grace helps us to endure. God's grace helps us stand still and see the salvation of the Lord when our situations are screaming at us to throw in the towel, quit, or separate. When we feel as though we're in desperate need of answers and directions, can I tell you that God's grace is sufficient, which means it is enough?

I teach a Bible study class every week. I remember one time my husband and I were having a real moment, once more, again. We had severe warfare going on between us, and I was heavy-laden as I tried my best to push past the trauma in the spirit. And it wasn't much of a surprise to me that I was in the midst of teaching the people of God about the sufficiency of God's grace. I could remember how I felt so desperate for God to come in and move by His Spirit so we could put the trial behind us. It didn't have that way. It seemed like the more I prayed about the problem, it kept staring us in the face. In the midst of my teaching the people of God about the grace of God, I seemed to be struggling. It goes without saying that the Lord spoke to me and said, "Adriene — My grace is sufficient for you as well." God told me in no uncertain terms, "If it's good enough for you to teach the people of God, it's also good enough for you to stand on in your marriage." OUCH! What He said to me was a bit shocking but nonetheless true. I totally agreed with what God said to me. I'm the kind of person who tries to live by the same word that I'm praying about, teaching and confessing to God and to others. I must be the first partaker of the Word of God that I share with others as I teach. Therefore, I had to take that same word and meditate on it to make my flesh behave and to bring it under subjection. I had to come to the place where I, myself, knew that regardless of how much the storm was raging, God wanted me to know that His grace was sufficient enough for me. He wanted me to know that His goodness, favor, and kindness toward me were enough to help me stand. God continued letting me know that His love for me was enough. That's powerful. I pray you are catching this in your spirit, because the Bible says that faith works by love. There is just something about when you know how much God loves you; that same love speaks and says to you, "If He loves me, surely He will take care of me."

There are many times during marriage challenges, the trials try to get us so overwhelmed in hopes of convincing us that grace and grace alone is not enough. In the heat of the battle, and when our hearts are broken, we believe that we prefer a resolve, allowing God to keep the grace. Some of us, we much rather have peace in our homes instead of grace. We begin thinking, "Where is God right about now?" Again, we began thinking that grace and grace alone would not suffice. Listen, God tells us that grace *is* enough while we're waiting for the manifestation to show up. God wants us to come to such a place of trusting in Him in our marriage, that His very presence in our lives is sufficient enough to help us to stand. Think about it! Knowing God's presence is always with you should be a great source of comfort. He has promised never to leave us or forsake us. His presence is our sustenance. How many of you can agree with me that nobody can keep you and sustain you as our God can? So, His presence should be enough to give us peace amid every raging storm. Selah! I want to encourage you, when it seems like you need something in addition to God's grace to help you stand, God's grace is sufficient until the manifestation of the promise shows up. God says, "Grace is enough!"

The Apostle Paul is a beautiful example of God's grace being enough. God allowed him to have a thorn in his flesh. Anybody familiar with this story knows that in 2 Corinthian in chapter 12, God took the Apostle Paul to the 3rd heaven. On this visit, God pulled back the curtains and allowed Paul to take a peek into glory. Now, Paul didn't know whether this was an inner-body or an out-of-body experience. On this visit, God began revealing some things to Paul that he says he was not able to express. They were unspeakable things, and things he declared were too sacred even to repeat. God showed him some revelations that the masses had never experienced before.

Therefore, in order to keep the Apostle Paul from getting the big head and getting all puffed up, God allowed the enemy to give him a thorn in the flesh. The Bible tells us in *2 Corinthians 12:7* how the messenger of Satan was sent to buffet him. God allowed the enemy to come, contend against, and battle with the Apostle Paul. The Bible never tells us what this thorn was, but it was a real source of aggravation.

In *2 Corinthians 12:8–9*, you will read the Apostle Paul saying, *"Concerning this I pleaded with the Lord three times that it might leave me; but He has said to me, My grace is sufficient for you [My loving-kindness and My mercy are more than enough — always available— regardless of the situation]; for [My] power is being perfected [and is completed and shows itself most effectively] in [your] weakness."* (AMP) Three times, the Apostle Paul sought the Lord to deliver him from this thorn. God's response to his prayer was "My grace is sufficient for you."

There will be plenty of times that you will seek God in prayer concerning your marriage, and instead of God removing the situation, He will tell you also about how His grace is enough. I like how God didn't leave the Apostle Paul hanging. He could have left him trying to figure out why God wouldn't remove the thorn. The Lord told him the very same thing He's telling us today. He's saying that His power is perfected in our times of weakness. He says His power is completed and shows itself most-effectively when we're at our weakest state. Therein lies the reason God did not remove the thorn. God's power is at its greatest when we are at our weakest. If I were you, I would read that again. God's power is made perfect in our weakness. The very place where our strength runs out is the same place where God's power begins to show up in our lives. I believe that there are so many times that God is trying to get us to come to the end of ourselves. He is trying to help us grow in Him as we learn how to depend upon Him.

A Handicap or a Gift

In *2 Corinthians 12:9*, I like how the scripture reads in the Message Bible. It says God told the Apostle Paul, *"My grace is enough; it's all you need. My strength comes into its own in your weakness."* The Apostle Paul goes on to say *"Once I heard that, I was glad to let it happen!"* (MSG) I think that is an absolutely powerful statement that most of us are not accustomed to hearing! Have you ever made that kind of statement concerning your trials and tribulations that "You were glad to let it happen," based upon the promises of God's Word? He went on to say, *"I quit focusing on the handicap and began appreciating the gift. It was a case of Christ's strength moving in on my weakness. Now I take limitations in stride, and with good cheer, these limitations that cut me down to size-abuse, accidents, opposition, bad breaks. I just let Christ take over! And so the weaker I get, the stronger I become."* (MSG) There is a lot to digest here. The Apostle Paul is telling us here that there was once a time while having to deal with the thorn, he looked at it like a handicap. He lookcd at the thorn as something that was holding him down and holding him back from progressing or moving forward. I'm still talking about marriage here. He looked at the thorn as something negative without any value attached to it at all. I can tell you that this principle applies across the board. When he realized what God was doing in and through this trial, it helped him to change his perspective. He then stopped looking at the thorn as a problem and as a handicap and began appreciating it as a gift. My Lord! He began looking at it as a growth-mechanism that would help his faith to grow stronger in God. Can we, in our walk with God, ever come to the place to be glad "Just let it happen," so God's strength and power in our lives will come into its own?

I know it's difficult to see a thorn as a gift. The word "handicap" means a circumstance that makes progress or success difficult. Somebody, you are reading this book right now and feel as if you cannot move forward in your marriage. You might feel as though having a happy and healthy marriage is beyond your reach. The devil is a liar. And yes, it is beyond your reach in the absence of God's power intervening. But, it is not outside God's omnipotent power to get you to that next level in your faith and, ultimately, in your marriage. In Matthew 19:23–24, Jesus was ministering to the disciples concerning how difficult it is for a rich man to get into heaven. After Jesus finished ministering to them concerning the subject, the Bible says that the disciples said, "My God, who then has any chance of entering?" They were saying it was impossible for a rich man to enter into heaven. Now, as it relates to marriage, I say to you the same thing that Jesus told the disciples. The Message Bible says Jesus said to them, *"No chance at all if you think you can pull it off by yourself. Every chance in the world if you trust God to do it."*

We fool ourselves if we trust our husband or wife to make the impossible possible in this life that we live. Sometimes, we put too much pressure on our mates, who can be powerful, yet human with limitations. Jesus says, *"With man this is impossible, but with God all things are possible."* (NIV) So, if it's been hard for you to move forward, or you feel like you've been stuck and stagnated, can I encourage you to stop looking at your challenge as a handicap? Right now, if you are experiencing a sense of defeat or hopelessness, take on the mindset of the Apostle Paul. In essence, it was as if he was saying, "I no longer want this thorn to be a sense of frustration and aggravation anymore. Therefore, I will change my perspective on how I'm looking at what I'm looking at, in my present situation. I no longer see it as a hindrance or as a disadvantage. My problem is no longer an obstacle for me, but it's a steppingstone for me." My friend, know that God allows it to take place for your good. While Satan means it for your demise, God uses it for your good. From this day forward, ask God to help you to start looking at every obstacle as a gift to move on to the next chapter in your marriage as opposed to a handicap.

<u>Pushed to My Knees</u>

Not only did the Apostle Paul show us that he started looking at the thorn as a gift, but he also said that all the enemy ended up doing was pushing him to his knees. If there is any place that our trials should drive us, it should be to our knees. It shouldn't just move us to another conversation to complain. It shouldn't drag us into an opportunity to magnify the wrong things. When the Apostle Paul was forced to deal with this thorn, the Message Bible says in *2 Corinthians 12:9 "Satan's angel did his best to get me down; what he in fact did was push me to my knees."*

The Apostle Paul said the enemy tried his best to get him down. But when all was said and done, and when all of the smoke settled, he realized what Satan had actually done was push him to his knees. If we can be honest with ourselves, God has to allow us to go through some things so the situation might push us to our knees. The Apostle Paul was basically saying was, *"All the enemy did was cause me to grab hold of*

God even the more." What he was saying is that the problem caused him to find his way even more into the presence of God. That's why the Bible says in *1 Corinthians 2:8* that *"If the princes of this world would have known what they were doing or had they known the outcome of the cross, they never would have crucified the Lord of Glory."* (paraphrased)

It's Your Way In

I don't think I will ever forget the words of one of my pastor's teachings. He always said, "What's in your way is your way in." This particular saying means that the very thing you're looking at as a source of frustration and aggravation is the same thing God is trying to use to propel you to that next level of faith. The enemy is trying to destroy your marriage, and the weapons he is using to torment your mind are the things God uses to get you to that next level. Always remember that what's in your way is your way in. I can personally testify to this truth. The reason is that I can recall the many times my husband and I came out and survived the attacks the enemy launched at us in order to disintegrate our marriage. After every episode, once we're able to regroup and get back in one accord, it seems as if our marriage grows to another level. Every time the enemy tried to make us think that we would not survive, "this time," as he supposed, we came back more robust and in love than we were, before we went into battle. It's weird how God allows spiritual warfare to bring out the best in us. I believe it's because when life squeezes you, whatever is in you will begin coming out of you. If you have the Word of God in you, at some point, the God in you has to rise to the occasion.

When God says "No," and when He refuses to remove the thorns (the source of aggravation) in our lives, He is allowing us to grow in our marriage relationship. I said it earlier and I will say it again. God allow trials in our lives so we can have a dependency upon Him. See, we have to be honest with ourselves to know that we wouldn't depend upon God as much, if we didn't need God as much. You can say amen to that!

We'll have to go through some things in life to grow. You can fast all you want, and you can pray all you want. You can petition God as much as you please while asking God to remove the source of frustration and aggravation that marriage can bring on, but the sufficiency of God's grace is enough. I know we don't like it. I know that it doesn't feel good, but He created us to need Him in life. We might want a new car, and we might want a new house, or a new pair of shoes, but WE NEED GOD! He fixed and orchestrated life so you and I will always and forever depend upon Him. And one thing I love about God is that even though He does not send everything that happens in life, He most definitely uses everything to help us to realize our dependency upon Him.

Never think marriages are supposed to work out for the better simply because that's what you desire. Don't ever think we just get to *go* to another level in God, but we must *grow* to another level. We don't just get to go forward, but we must be willing to grow forward. We cannot go over it.

We cannot go under it, and we cannot go around the process, but we must go through the process of growth. The process does not have to be hard all of the time, but it is a process that has the capability of yielding some beautiful results if we allow God's grace to be enough.

Overtaken in a fault

In the same manner that God so gracious restores us to our rightful place in Him when we fall short of His glory, He also expects us to restore our spouses when they fall short. *Galatians 6:1–4 says, "Brothers, if anyone is caught in any sin, you who are spiritual [that is, you who are responsive to the guidance of the Spirit] are to restore such a person in a spirit of gentleness [not with a sense of superiority or self-righteousness], keeping a watchful eye on yourself, so that you are not tempted as well. Carry one another's burdens and in this way you will fulfill the requirements of the law of Christ [that is, the law of Christian love]. For if anyone thinks he is something [special] when [in fact] he is nothing [special except in his own eyes], he deceives himself. But each one must carefully scrutinize his own word [examining his actions, attitudes, and behavior] and then he can have the personal satisfaction and inner joy of doing something commendable without comparing himself to another."*

I believe every married couple should read and meditate on these scriptures. When the enemy has stepped in during those times of distress, mistakes, errors, or sins, it's a good thing if one of us, if not both of us, are listening to and hearing from God. I pray that this resonates with you. If I can go a bit further, God is saying the one who is responsive to the Word of God, and the one who is operating in the fruit of the Spirit should be the one to lift their mate. But woe unto that couple in the midst of a spiritual battle where neither one of you is responsive to the voice of God or the leading of the Spirit of God. I'm sure that we've all been in that position as well.

I want to labor on this point because this is something that is very challenging for many couples to grasp. Again, the Word of God tells us that if either of us is caught in sin or is overtaken by a fault, the one who is open and sensitive to the Spirit of God has been given the greater obligation and responsibility at that time to restore our mate. If we endeavor to obey God's Word and keep the bond of unity, these scriptures talk about what we, as mature believers, should do when we encounter others who are overtaken in sin or a fault. This scripture is not only speaking about others who aren't a part of our family unit, but it also definitely includes our spouses. I pray that this resonates with you.

The unfortunate truth of the matter is that there will be plenty of times in marriage when sins and faults will overtake us both. To be overtaken is when sin, passion, or temptation comes upon a person and gets the better of them. It's when sin or temptation comes upon an individual suddenly, or even not so suddenly, but it gets the best of them and causes them to be overtaken or held captive by its grip. So, in marriage, the person who is more in touch and in tune with God and is presently responding to the prompting of the Spirit of God, is the one to restore. The stronger partner is commanded to uplift the weaker partner. By the power of the Holy Spirit, the stronger is to help return their mate to their former condition, place, or position in God's kingdom. Help that person recover from their errors and faults from the grip of sin and temptation. That's what grace will help you to do. We go wrong in our relationship when we are convinced that we have been wronged, or treated so harshly, that we begin looking for the offending party to return and restore. We look for them to come back with their tail between their legs, apologizing to get it right with us. Don't get me wrong, it's good if they do, but God calls upon the stronger one to make it right.

Oftentimes, the offending party will be too overtaken by their fault or wrongdoing to return to do the restoration. We tend to forget that the offender is in need of being repaired. The offender is in desperate need of the Spirit of God to lift them into their rightful place before they can operate correctly. When we obey this commandment to restore, we are given an opportunity to see what the grace of God looks like, and how grace operates.

God also gives us the insight on how the restoration should be carried out. He tells us to restore without feeling a sense of superiority or self-righteousness. You know, it becomes easy for us to see ourselves as self-righteous if we're not keeping a watchful eye on ourselves. It's elementary to become haughty, self-righteous, and holier than thou while we're pointing our fingers at others, especially our spouses. God tells us to restore that person with a spirit of humility. When we restore someone with the spirit of humility, we must restore without being full of anger and we must not be unforgiving. Rather, we should restore with kindness and forbearance. We must carry it out with much love and with much compassion. We cannot restore them by hollering and screaming. Don't try to correct them while cursing at them. Restore with much patience and endurance because love endures all things. Be able to be tolerant of that person because, after all, God tolerates us all day, every day. It's hard to restore someone when we have a terrible temper and are intolerant of others' faults and behaviors. We will never be able to be instrumental in helping others to regain their rightful place if we ourselves are overtaken in the sin of anger and self-righteousness. It will be counter-productive if we try to restore our mates if we haven't yet learned how to bridle our tongue or if we are not walking in humility and the love of God. I know that I'm talking well here. Restoring our spouses must be carried out with God's help through grace. We should be willing to exercise the Golden Rule found in *Matthew 7:12, which says, "So then, in everything treat others the same way you want them to treat you."*

Finally, when it comes down to restoration, we must know how to love the person while hating the sin and the fault that overtook them in the first place. Many people and married couples alike have yet to learn how to separate a person from the sin they commit. Thank God that He does not hold us over hell's fire when we are overtaken in a fault. He knows how to separate His love for us from the very sins that we commit against Him. Now, that's love!

<u>Love Covers</u>

1 Peter 4:8 says, "Above all, have fervent and unfailing love for another because love covers a multitude of sins." (AMP) But yet another translation says *"Love throws a veil over a multitude of faults."* (Weymouth New Testament) Now that's good. This is grace in action. How willing are we to throw a veil over our spouse's faults when they fall short of the glory of God? When we throw a veil over our spouse's sins, faults, and shortcomings, we are willing to cover, conceal, and hide their imperfections, flaws, and defects. It means that you have to be willing to *overlook* some things. It means that we must know how to *walk by* and *walk past* some things while making our way to our knees to let our requests be made known to God, and not every single time to our spouses. *Psalms 103:10 says, "He has not dealt with us according to our sins [as we deserve], Nor rewarded us [with punishment] according to our wickedness."* Will somebody say, "Oh, for Grace!" God commands us to carry one another's burdens. By God's grace, we can help our mates overcome the hindrances and hurdles of life, which will, on many occasions, spill over into our marriage. He holds back from us that which we do deserve, and He gives us that which we do not deserve, all because He is willing to cover us many times. I will say it again — that's love! Aren't you glad about that? I'm so grateful to God that He does not give me my just reward when I have transgressed against Him. I understand that some things are quite complicated to get over when we have been wronged, which is quite understandable. God knows! If you have made up your mind to move forward, ask God to heal and help you so you won't be stagnated. It isn't easy to *go over* that which we cannot seem to *get over!*

Finally, while learning how to operate in grace, you must know that it is not necessary to feel the need to right every wrong that's been done against you. You don't have to act out or respond when you have been offended by your spouse. When we get to the place in marriage where we believe that we're going to get our spouses straight and we're going to put them in their place, that's the time we have taken on the role of God. We are not God, and I have never read a scripture in the Bible where God sent out a request where He was looking for any assistant god to help Him to be God — have you? My friend, it is my prayer that you know beyond a shadow of a doubt that you can stand on the promises of God in your marriage, because He is faithful to whom he has promised. God is so wonderful and so awesome. I leave you with this — when mercy says, "no," know that the grace of God still says, "yes." I want you to know that when you feel as if you are at the end of your rope in marriage, and it seems as if you have passed the breaking point, God assures you that His grace will help you to stand. His amazing grace is sufficient, and His grace is most definitely enough!

WHAT GOD HAS JOINED TOGETHER

I could remember the day that Shawn and I first met. Even though it was over thirty-one years ago, all the details surrounding our union are fresh and vivid in my mind. When we first met, as I stated earlier, I was not a born-again believer. Before I gave my life to the Lord, one night, as my good friend and I were headed to the nightclub, we realized we didn't have enough money for drinks. She said, "Let's go by this guy I know, Shawn, and get some money." That was the best house visit I have ever had. So, we were headed to his house, and after about a ten-minute visit, we were on our way to the club for some drinks and to dance the night away. Shawn was a bartender at the club that we were attending. After initially meeting Shawn that night, some years passed when we didn't see each other. Initially, I didn't know he was attracted to me the first night we met until I saw him looking at me several times from my peripheral vision during those ten minutes at the house.

I must say that when we first met, I was having a really rough time in my life, but I don't know if I was quite looking for a boyfriend or a husband at the time. Therefore, the looks didn't faze me at all. I think it was because I was trying my best to numb the pain of being lost with no direction in life. After a few years had gone by, my friend and I were still hanging out in nightclubs. One night, as we were headed back to that same club, to my surprise, Shawn was bartending at the club. As I sat there at the bar, watching the people dance with the psychedelic lights flashing, I noticed how he kept flirting with me in between mixing drinks for other patrons. This time, I too was flirting back with him. You know, it was all in the eyes! And with the biggest smile on his face, he said to me, "Where are we going this weekend?" That was his pickup line. I guess it worked, because this time, I was doing cartwheels on the inside while keeping a straight face. Trying to keep my cool, I said, "I don't know. Where would you like to go?" I answered. By that weekend, we had our first date. I'm not quite sure how our first date ended up being at the mall. I guess it was as good of a place as any. While in the mall, he kept taking me in and out of stores, asking me if I wanted him to buy me anything. And with every offer, I said "No." After we got married, we would often laugh about that first date. The reason being is he stated to me that when I kept telling him "no" as it related to buying me something, he said he knew I was the woman for him. You see, he was making really good money and testing me to see if I was all about the money, or if I genuinely like him as a person. I'm so glad that I passed the money test!

After we married, I remembered how he would often share the story about when he was away in the Army after we first met, how a gentleman asked him if he had a girlfriend. Initially, he said he told the guy "no." After a few seconds went by, he said that the Spirit of God touched him, and he told the guy, "Yes! I do have a girlfriend. Her name is Adriene." As soon as he returned to New Orleans, his quest began as he frantically began looking for me— everywhere! Anybody and everybody whom he remotely thought knew me or even knew of me, he would ask them where he could find me. He would always say it was God who kept putting me in his heart that gave him a knowing that I was meant to be his wife. What a mighty God we serve! And to this day, I can still say that I am so blessed because that was the beginning of something so wonderful. We were married about nine months later.

It bears repeating that if we had to travel down this journey all over again, we both have declared to one another that we would do it all over again. I'm talking about in and through all of the good, the bad, and the ugly. We would do it all over again to get to where we are now. I can testify to the fact that through all of the rough patches in our marriage, I can truly say the good times far outweigh all the learning moments. All of the ups have outweighed the downs. I love him with all of my heart. I wouldn't want to do life with anyone else. We both believe that God has joined us together beyond a shadow of a doubt.

Shawn and I are soul mates. It's amazing how we think the very same thoughts at times. I am even more excited about the fact that we still excite one another. Most of the time, we still laugh, hug and kiss. I still sit on his lap and long for him to hold me tight. It's the Lord's doing, and it's marvelous in my eyes. One of the things that blessed me the most is even when I didn't know the Lord, and he was a backslider, God loved us so much, that He saw fit to join us together, because He is Alpha and Omega. Isn't it good to know that God sees so much further up the road than we ever could? Not only did God see our past and future, but more importantly, God knew He would ultimately join us together as one.

Mark 10:6 says, "But from the beginning of the creation God MADE THEM MALE AND FEMALE. FOR THIS REASON A MAN SHALL LEAVE HIS FATHER AND HIS MOTHER [to establish a home with his wife], AND THE TWO SHALL BECOME ONE FLESH; So that they are no longer two, but [are united as] one flesh. Therefore, what God has united and joined together, man must not separate [by divorce]." (AMP)

God speaks about the importance of man and woman coming together as one in the Old Testament and the New Testament. Oneness in marriage is God's idea. I want to touch upon the area of a man leaving his father and his mother. When God says a man should leave his father and mother and cleave to his wife, God is telling the man that he must leave the home of his parents. After marriage, God gave the man the responsibility of providing a dwelling place for him and his wife to dwell in safely. It does not mean that he could no longer give assistance of any kind to his parents. It doesn't mean he is not to care for them in any way, shape, or form just because he is married. And despite the popular belief of some, leaving the parents does not consist of him turning his back on them for his bride. I have had many conversations with people who would love nothing more than their mates to cut the parents of their lives totally. I know some parents can be challenging to deal with, but I believe that allows God to create even more incredible opportunities to show others the love of God in our lives, if at all possible. As parents age, their children should be there to assist them in the various ways that they need assistance. Again, leaving the parents' home means he must have the wherewithal to provide a roof over her head and to care for her.

Therefore, this calls for him to leave his parents' dwelling place. Not only must he leave his parents' home, but he must be willing to cleave to his wife. When a man cleaves to his wife, it means his allegiance must first and foremost belong to his wife, before and above all others. After marriage, he must be glued to her and stick with her as they begin life together. The wife must also have this same responsibility in sticking with her husband as she has been called by his side to be his helpmate. As stated in *Ephesians 5:25, his job should be to love his wife "even as Christ also loved the church and gave Himself for it."* (KJ21) He should constantly wash her with God's Word so that he may present her to himself as a glorious church. She must always be in the process of concerning herself with helping him to become the man of God that God has called him to be in life. He should love her even as he loves himself. *Ephesians 5:33* tells us that *"the wife see that she reverence her husband."* (KJV) The amplified Bible says, *"She [must see to it] that she respects and delights in her husband [that she notices him and prefers him and treats him with loving concern, treasuring him, honoring him, and holding him dear]."*

As couples strive to become one in everyday life, they must work hard to achieve unity in their marriage. Being unified in marriage does not mean that God has called either of them to lose their identity in one another. When they both know who they are, they would see that they are still two unique individuals who both bring much to the table, while at the same time, continuing to be one spiritually in the eyes of God. When a man and his wife come to a place of unity, it further means that they are joined together and are connected to one another more than they are connected to others.

I have personally seen and heard of real-life situations when a man leaves his parents, and even after leaving, they still give their parents an authoritative voice over their wives. And by the same token, many wives who have become one flesh with their spouses have been guilty of being deceived by valuing the opinions and the advice of their parents, friends, and confidantes above their husbands. There are also times when wives have allowed their children to come in and dethrone the position of authority that God has placed the husband in as it relates to marriage. We, as married couples, are not married to our children because, one day, children will grow up and leave. We are married to our mates, and they must have our first allegiance outside of God. We must know how to cleave to our spouses. That's why the scripture says, *"What God has joined together, let no man put asunder."* The word "asunder" means a pulling apart, disjoining, or disuniting. We should never allow anyone to pull our marriages apart by dividing and dismantling them for any reason.

I want to say here that we, as married individuals, should also strive not to put asunder what God has joined together. I believe that far too often, when someone reads that scripture, they are under the impression or assume that God is speaking to outsiders or simply to other people. How many of you have read that scripture and inserted yourself in it? We too, must strive on an individual level not to allow the enemy to come in and disunite, dismantle, and separate us by being ignorant of the devil's devices. We must be wise because the Bible tells us that the enemy is very cunning. And often, if we don't have a spirit of discernment, the enemy will be operating right under our noses to destroy us, while many couples don't have a clue as to what is taking place. Ask God to give you the spirit of discernment. But, if I can add to that, knowing God's Word is the greatest weapon and the most remarkable tool we can use to safeguard our marriages.

Let No One Put Asunder

I recall one time my husband and I were having a gut-wrenching challenge in our marriage. Quite naturally, my flesh told me to run and get away for a few days until the smoke settled. Once more again, I decided to stay and fight the enemy, not my husband, in my own home on my own turf, as opposed to a hotel room or my sister's house. As the battle was raging, I could remember reading so much material to help my marriage in the midst of my pain and my heartache. One night as I tried so desperately to get some sleep after lying in bed for three hours with all kinds of thoughts running through my head, I turned over and picked up my phone. I ran across this story that left me so heartbroken concerning one Christian couple's marriage. The couple had been married for quite some time. Somewhere along the way, the husband ended up committing adultery. After a time of being separated, they decided to get back together again to work at reuniting the marriage. Now the wife stated that she had some serious trust issues because her trust had been broken and because she felt so violated. Despite that, there they were, announcing to their friends, their loved ones, and practically anyone who would listen that they were back together and prayerful in their quest to reunite. After some time had passed, the husband began to fall short again in the area of adultery. The wife spoke about her complete and utter devastation. She said she absolutely loved her husband with everything in her and prayed so earnestly to God to make the marriage work. As they struggled to find healing and reconciliation, the husband was unwilling to change so the marriage might be saved.

In marriage, don't be surprised if you experience that regardless of how much or how hard one spouse loves their mate, it does not automatically mean that the other spouse will reciprocate the same amount of love or the same level of commitment. Unfortunately, in this case, we can see that regardless of how much one spouse can try to make things work out for the better, the sad truth is that we cannot control someone else's will. Regardless of how much we love our spouses, we cannot make someone do right, live right, or walk upright before God. We have to know that the commitment of one is no guarantee of a commitment being reciprocated. I also want you to know that, as believers, we are not exempt from falling short of the glory of God. Anytime a born-again believer allows the enemy to deceive them at any given point in their walk with God or have a lapse in judgment, you can best believe the enemy is standing right there to capitalize off the shortcoming. Not only that, but anytime we lose our connection with God, we become vulnerable, becoming a prime enemy target. Therefore, when we walk in rebellion and disobedience, there is an open portal that we have created for the enemy to enter. When we are not connected to *"THE REAL POWER SOURCE,"* as one of my mentors would always say, know that the enemy is coming in to shame you and destroy your witness and your testimony. He wants to try to discredit you in all you stand for as a believer. He is always seeking out and searching for an opportunity to cause what has been done in the dark to come to light so he may give the church, which is the body of Christ, a black eye. Being obedient is for our safety and our good—that is why we are called to be people of wisdom. As I stated earlier, the Bible warns us that the enemy is very cunning. Many times, we are not aware of the tricks and the schemes he uses to come in to try to dismantle and destroy our marriages.

This lovely couple that I previously spoke about earlier ended up getting a divorce because what God joined together, the enemy was allowed to come in and dismantle and caused there to be a divorce.

Can We Talk About It

Another thing we must also be mindful of is that when God says, "Let no man put asunder," we must know that when we refuse to communicate with our spouses concerning essential issues, we are guilty of causing our marriages to be dismantled. A lack of communication is an open portal for the enemy to get a foothold into the marriage. Sometimes, we are unaware of how we are instrumental in destroying our marriages due to a lack of communication. Because, slowly but surely, when we don't communicate to find a resolution to the issues that are challenging the marriage, we are allowing the enemy to come in to *"Divide and Conquer."* It is not wise to keep covering up issues that are screaming out for some attention. At some point in our marriage, we must be willing to address the elephant in the room, lest we continue to kick the bucket farther up the road. A lack of communication is not a sign of a healthy marriage. Refusing to communicate is also not a sign of someone who wants their marriage to go and grow to another level. I find that a lack of communication amongst couples is one of the greatest things that keep married couples divided. It keeps them from becoming one as God desires them to be, even though they are one spiritually. The truth of the matter is plenty of individuals do not know how or aren't willing to communicate. And that can be for many different reasons. It can be because one or both spouses are unwilling to change. I find that many people do not want to deal with themselves when it comes down to flaws and shortcomings. It has always baffled me, and it is quite interesting when we desire our mates to deal with us, but in all actuality, we are not willing to deal with ourselves. If you want your mate to deal with you, first, be ready to deal with yourself. God just said something right there. Be open to change. Because, in every healthy marriage, you can best believe that there will be many "Come-to-Jesus-moments," that must take place if the couple wants a chance to beat the marriage statistics. Say amen to that! Therefore, it is imperative for us to learn how to deal with ourselves before God has to step in and deal with us in ways that are pretty uncomfortable to us and in ways we really do not like. God does chasten those whom He loves.

Another reason for the lack of communication is that one spouse is always left feeling like "the victim" during the communication efforts. We must always be careful and mindful saying, "You, you, you! You did this or you did that." We must know how to change our dialogue when we're trying to communicate. And then, some individuals in a marriage find communication quite difficult because they suffer from anger issues. And because they suffer from anger or anger that begins to manifest itself into a rage, they know how easy it is for them to go from zero to one hundred in a matter of seconds. Therefore, they shut down and refuse to talk. A lack of communication helps no one. Remember, if we are not a part of the solution, then by default, we have become a part of the problem.

Now that we understand how God has commanded us to stay together and joined as one, there has to come a time in the marriage that if we *cannot* or *will not* be willing to communicate effectively with the other, that's the time when the couple should consider going to a marriage counselor. We have to be willing to admit that we need help. *Proverbs 11:2 says, "When pride comes [boiling up with an arrogant attitude of self-importance], then come dishonor and shame, But with the humble [the teachable who have been chiseled by trial and who have learned to walk humbly with God] there is wisdom and soundness of mind." Proverbs 11:14 says, "Where there is no [wise, intelligent] guidance, the people fall [and go off course like a ship without a helm], But in the abundance of [wise and godly] counselors there is victory."*

Can I tell you that God never intended for us to be some "Lone Ranger" couple or a "Lone Ranger" individual on an island by ourselves? In other words, God has given us and has made available to us godly and professional people who can help us along the way by helping to keep our marriages intact. We have to be willing to humble ourselves. We must be willing and ready to say, "It's me, oh Lord. I'm the one who is standing in need of prayer." One of the greatest reasons people don't want to go to a counselor, even when they see their marriages falling apart, is from a spirit of pride. I get it. Humbling ourselves is not the easiest thing to do, though it is the necessary thing to do, especially if you desire to stay married, that is. Remember that *Proverbs 16:18* says, *"Pride goes before destruction, and a haughty spirit before a fall."* The Message Bible gives us an even clearer understanding of how detrimental pride is to the one who continues to operate in it. *Proverbs 16:18 says, "First pride, then the crash — the bigger the ego, the harder the fall."* OUCH! It is never a good thing to operate in a spirit of pride.

Another scripture that comes to me as I share the Word of God is found in *Proverbs 1:7,* which says, *"The fear of the LORD is the beginning of knowledge, but fools despise wisdom and instruction."* The word "fear" is not the kind of fear that makes an individual afraid, tormented, or paranoid. The word "fear" in this particular text means to have a reverence for God. When we have reverence for God, we respect Him. We admire Him, praise Him, honor Him, and adore Him. I don't know about you, but I have a deep affection for the LORD! I reverence Him. Where there is a lack of reverence for God, there you will find an absence of knowledge, because reverence is the beginning of a person being able to come into the kind of wisdom and knowledge that will help them to live right. Say "Amen!" The fear of the Lord is what we need to help us know which turns and directions to make in life, lest we find ourselves in a ditch. The fear of the Lord allows us to make the right decisions so we can benefit from the promises of God that cannot fail. Therefore, when one turns their back on acquiring wisdom and instructions, the Bible calls that person a fool. I didn't say that, but God did. I need all of the understanding, knowledge, and instructions that I can get to keep a healthy marriage that brings glory to God and inner peace to my husband and me.

Going back to that previous scripture, I want you to know that if the Bible says that a fool hates instructions, that means that a fool will remain in his folly. Therefore, when it comes down to the marital relationship, the person who continues to rebel is no longer willing to learn so they may become better, which in turn, means that they have accepted having a marriage that is held captive by the grips of the enemy. If we are too prideful to receive wise counsel so that our marriages will not entirely fall apart or even end up in divorce, we have to get to the place where we are willing to reach beyond ourselves to get what we need. When someone is drowning, they don't care who throws out the lifeline. All they know is that they want to live, so it does not matter who is pulling them to safety or who has come to the rescue. You have to catch that. I am saying that there are too many people out there who are already where we are trying to go in our marriage. There are too many people who have "been there and done that." Not only did they get the t-shirt, but they also still have their marriages intact simply because they weren't too proud to ask for "Help." Therefore, it is no longer about "How," but it becomes about "Who?" Who can help my marriage get to that next level?

Regularly Scheduled Maintenance

As of now, I have a 2015 black Toyota Camry. I call her "My baby." I do not covet my vehicle, but I tell you, I am always thanking God for my vehicle. I am proud of how I kept her up.

Ever since I purchased my vehicle in August 2015, I made sure that I always took my car in for regularly scheduled maintenance jobs. I kept my oil changes up to date. I made sure when they told me my brake pads were beginning to wear down, I made an appointment to come back in to ensure my car continued running as smoothly as possible. I can say that because I did my part, my car does its part. And yes, it cost me something. Many times, it cost me *A LOT!* And if the truth be told, there were sometimes my checking account wasn't where I wanted it to be, but I still made the sacrifice anyway because I knew if I did not take care of my car that my car would not take care of me. After having my vehicle for over seven years, it hasn't broken down on me once, except for a flat tire due to me rolling over a nail. In seven years, it has always started when I put the key in the ignition. In seven years, it has always taken me to my intended destination without me ever being broken down on the side of the road. My vehicle continues to perform well because I have a "Whatever-it-takes attitude" toward caring for it. I am willing to pay the price to keep it in top-notch condition. As I previously stated, it cost me something. I work hard in my marriage to try to adapt that same attitude in my marriage. If I can have that kind of attitude for something that is material, how much more should I adapt that kind of attitude for that which is holy in the eyes of God!

How much of a price are you willing to pay in order to keep your marriage in top-notch condition? Do you have a "Whatever-it-takes" attitude in your marriage so that you won't be instrumental in putting asunder what God has joined together? You must have a readiness to pay the price. And often, my friend, the price you pay will have to be paid with humility. The cost of staying together often requires you to give God a "YES" when everything in you is screaming "NO!" Sometimes, you will literally have to pay the price with tears, along with sacrificing yourself as you press to obey the will of God. Hey, let's not kid ourselves here — there is a hefty cost and a hefty price tag that God will require of you after He has joined you together. The price a couple must pay in marriage is the reason that marriage is not for the faint at heart. Always remember in the eyes of God, you two are one, and God expects us to live our lives accordingly. Once again, God gives us a command that what He has orchestrated and ordained, let no one come in-between to cause separation or divorce — and that means us as well!

The Process of Becoming

The very process of becoming can be laborious when the Bible talks about how two shall become one. It's the becoming part that will test every fiber of our being. The process alone can sometimes make you feel as if you are in an endless war. When you are in the process of becoming, don't be surprised if one of you finds yourself sleeping on the couch. Don't be surprised if one of you finds yourself sleeping in the spare bedroom. The process alone has driven some couples to divorce court. Becoming can be incredibly challenging for a newly married couple and sometimes couples who have been married for a spell, simply because you two come from different backgrounds. You have a different set of beliefs. You have different mindsets and different ways of seeing things. The two of you were probably raised totally differently with your spiritual upbringing or lack thereof. And then there's God, right there in the middle, trying to get you two to become one. What a process!

I have been married only once. Therefore, I have never experienced a divorce. When I speak with people who have gone through a divorce, they tell me divorce is an excruciating and painful process. I believe that to be true because it's tough when a couple goes through a divorce, simply because they have spent so much time and effort trying to become one. Some of them have invested so much of themselves into the marriage in trying to become soul mates. So, after becoming one, when or if they start moving forward to do an about-face, meaning trying to get out of the marriage, it is an arduous and painful process. It's heartbreaking because there is a tearing of the soul that has been bonded together spiritually. It's painful to rip apart one soul and cause it to start operating again as two. As I have shared with several people, after divorce, they still find it quite challenging to let go of what was shared between the couple. Some couples may wonder why it's so hard to let go after divorce, but it's because the bond that was shared was created by God. The bond was a God-given bond, because in the mind of God, marriage was always meant to be for keeps.

I once read an article describing how God feels about divorce. It said divorce is compared to having an amputation. It's like cutting away a part of the body or amputating it. Therefore, if God says the two shall become one flesh, divorce is like cutting away at the body for many. And I believe we all know that there are many times that divorce or *amputation* isn't always warranted based on God's Word. Divorce will never accomplish God's intended purpose of marriage, whether they were justified or not. I want to say that even if a couple gets a divorce — warranted or unwarranted, God is still the God of all love, and He is a forgiving God.

I have watched many couples go through separation and divorce, and it's tough to watch. God is able to keep you! God can navigate your marriage through the rough terrain of becoming one. Based on the circumstances, I believe if a couple would stay in faith long enough, believing God to grow and to mature the union, God can sustain the longevity of the relationship. Of course, that's if both individuals are willing and obedient to God's Word. I am absolutely amazed at what God has done in my marriage. I give all praises to Him. We must have the willingness and the patience to stand the test of time. Growing in oneness does not take place overnight. Growth is growth, however long the process takes. I am a witness that the rewards of patiently waiting on God are so worth the wait.

The growth process in marriages often reminds me of when a mother is in childbirth. The agony of childbirth for some can be a very challenging and agonizing experience. However, when the baby is born, the pain that she endured in giving birth cannot be compared to the joy she experiences at the arrival of her baby. Just understand that in marriage, we never arrive. Therefore, I encourage you to keep getting up every day with a recommitment to commit again. Every day, go right back to the drawing board because every day presents new opportunities to grow to a new level in marriage. Therefore, I encourage you to *PUSH!*

The Commanded Blessing

"Behold, how good and how pleasant it is for brethren to dwell together in unity!" That is what the Psalmist David declares in *Psalms 133:1.* Being in one accord and being united with other believers carries much weight with God because it gives Him glory. It is also such a wonderful thing to be in one accord in marriage, and it is something that should be treasured and admired. I don't know about you, but I love peace. I thrive most in life and marriage when I am at peace. That's why I don't mind trying harder to keep the peace by walking in humility instead of pride. I, myself, am a peacemaker. And because of such, when my peace is disturbed through

marital chaos and confusion, it really does something to my entire being — spirit, soul, and body.

I am going to read *Psalms 133* in its entirety in the Message Bible. (1-3) says, *"How wonderful, how beautiful, when brothers and sisters get along! It's like costly anointing oil flowing down head and beard, Flowing down Aaron's beard, flowing down the collars of his priestly robes. It's like the dew on Mount Hermon flowing down the slopes of Zion. Yes, that's where GOD commands the blessing, ordains eternal life."*

As I did some studying about God commanding the blessing in the place of unity, I discovered that the blessing is not commanded any time God finds people in one accord or being unified. In Genesis, chapter 11, when the people decided they were going to unify and come together to build the Tower of Babel, God did not command the blessing. In fact, God showed up to stop and dismantle what they were trying to do, because even though they were in one accord, they were coming together to carry out a selfish task for a selfish purpose. Their motives were all wrong. They wanted to make a name for themselves. In the Amplified Bible, *Genesis 11:6, God says, "Behold, they are one [unified] people, and they all have the same language."* But God also went on to say, *"This is only the beginning of what they will do [in rebellion against Me], and now no evil thing they imagine they can do will be impossible for them."* So, this tells us that God does not always command blessings because people are unified.

Whenever we decide to come together in one accord to carry out the will of God, it's in that place where we will see God commands a blessing. If we desire God's commanded blessings, we must ensure that all our actions and efforts are being carried out so that God's kingdom will come, and His will shall be done on earth even as it is in heaven. When we come together for all the right reasons and the proper purposes, God will most definitely command a blessing. As we come together in one accord, our marriages will be blessed. My prayer for every person who reads this book is that you would indeed have a good understanding concerning the will of God for your life and your marriage. And when you do, as you allow God to have His way and let Him be LORD, your life and your marriage will blossom and flourish. If you want a healthy marriage, you must always be mindful of God's commanded blessing in the place of unity. Always remember when God says to us — *"What He Has Joined Together, Let No Man Put Asunder"* — that includes you! I am rooting for you!

IS OUT EVER AN OPTION?

—————⟨⊱❈⊰⟩—————

As the subtopic of this book states, I wholeheartedly believe that "Marriage Should Be For Keeps!" Unfortunately, marriages can, and many of them do end in divorce. When God designed marriage, it was always His original desire and intent for married couples to stay in a marriage covenant — *permanently!* A marriage covenant is considered to be an agreement. It means that two people have come together, in agreement with one another and with God. When a couple enters into a marriage covenant, they are agreeing to live by certain rules and abide by specific guidelines solely based upon God's Word. The covenant means that both spouses are willing to make the Word of God the final authority in their marriage! A marriage covenant, in the eyes of God means that we stood before each other and before Him, stating we were willing to stay together for better or for worse. We agreed that we are all in, whether we're experiencing the good or the bad during the course of the marital relationship. We further agreed and made a vow that said in sickness or in health, we would stay the course until death do us part. Therefore, the agreement goes beyond two people signing their names on the dotted line, witnessed by a pastor or a priest. A covenant is a spiritual matter, and therefore, it is spiritually binding. Marriage should not be entered into lightly. It takes God! God must be interwoven between every fiber of the marriage union.

It is amazing to me how the topic of whether God allows divorce only in certain situations or whether He allows divorce at all, is surrounded by such great controversy. You might not think it is, but over the years, there have been people who asked me this same question concerning marriage. I have had conversations with people who consisted of born-again believers as well as non-believers. I've had discussions with those who are married and those who aren't married. And to my surprise, what I have found is that many born-again believers wholeheartedly believe that God does not allow divorce for *any* reason at all! After being asked about my specific thoughts concerning if there is an out in marriage as far as God is concerned, first and foremost, the answer to this question is not, and never will be based upon what I believe or what I think about the subject matter. As a born-again believer, though I am not perfect, I try my best to live my life solely based on the Word of God, regardless of what I think or how I feel about it. Every day, I work hard at trying to allow God's Word to be the final authority in my life. Therefore, I cannot add to God's Word, nor can I take anything away from it.

So, precisely what does God says in the Word of God regarding *"Is Out Ever an Option?"* Is out ever an option for married couples who are in a spiritually binding covenant? Before we begin to dismantle the Word concerning that subject matter, I want you to know that I am writing this final chapter with heaviness of heart and with much prayer. For, I understand that there is someone who is reading this book and they are at their wit's end, and at this very moment, they are contemplating on calling it quits. I understand that some are holding this book in their hands whose hearts have been shattered into what seems to be a million little pieces. You desperately want to know what God has to say about what you are going through and the pain you are presently experiencing. There is a couple right now who is separated, and you're on the fence about what to do next as your marriage and your future hangs in the balance. You are unsure of your future. And finally, for someone who is reading, you are in the midst of painful divorce proceedings, or you have already gone through the process and are having doubts, wondering if you did the right thing. So, I say to you that based upon the Word of God, there is an out when it comes down to marriage. There are reasons God allows divorce to take place in the marriage relationship. I will now go over those reasons God allows an out.

Sexual Infidelity

So, let's cut to the chase. Let's be clear here. When it comes down to ending a marriage in divorce, out is an option based on *certain* circumstances. According to God's Word, there are two biblically based reasons God allows divorce. One of these two reasons listed in the Word of God is given by the Apostle Paul. He states that he speaks on abandonment because the Lord did not speak on the subject. *2 Peter 1:20 says, "But understand this first of all, that no prophecy of Scripture is a matter of or comes from one's own [personal or special] interpretation."* (AMP) The Apostle Paul was inspired by God when he spoke about Abandonment. In this final chapter, I will also touch upon another very important topic as well as a reason that can and often does leads to divorce.

The two reasons found in the Word of God that give an out for marriage are "Sexual Infidelity" and "Abandonment." First, let's talk about divorce due to the sin of sexual infidelity or immorality. In *Matthew 19:3 it says, "And Pharisees came to Jesus, testing Him and asking, 'Is it lawful for a man to divorce his wife for just any reason?' He replied, 'Have you never read that*

He who created them from the beginning mad them male and female , and said, "For this reason a man shall leave his father and mother and shall be joined inseparably to his wife, and the two shall become one flesh?" (AMP) So, they are no longer two, but one flesh. Therefore, what God has joined together, let no one separate.' The Pharisees said to Him, 'Why then did Moses command us to give her a certificate of divorce and send her away?' He said to them, 'Because your hearts were hard and stubborn, Moses permitted you to divorce your wives; but from the beginning it has not been this way. I say to you, whoever divorces his wife, except for sexual immorality, and marries another woman commits adultery.'"

Back in those days, women were not allowed to divorce their husbands, so Moses allowed the men to give their wives a certificate of divorce. So, when you read *Matthew 19:9*, the Bible tells us that *"A divorce can be granted due to sexual immorality."* Sexual infidelity is another name for unfaithfulness or adultery that can be carried out by one spouse or both spouses. Sadly, in today's culture, sex is flaunted, advertised, and welcomed everywhere. It can be readily seen at the playground, on television, on the big screen in movie theaters, in the grocery store, at the gym, and yes, even on the front row of the church house. Sexual infidelity or adultery is one of Satan's greatest weapons that he uses to destroy the sanctity of a marriage covenant. In *2 Corinthians 2:11, the Bible tells us that we cannot be ignorant or ignore the schemes and the devices of the enemy. If we ignore the device of sexual perversion, the enemy will get an advantage over us.*

Sex is a device that has been used more often than not to wreak havoc in a marriage and is the "guilty party" in having sent many vulnerable couples heading for divorce court. And, if by chance, the couple tries working it out, which some do, it's a long uphill journey in dealing with the trust that has been destroyed due to unfaithfulness. Now, I would be remiss if I didn't tell you that God is able to do all things. Many couples whose marriages have been attacked with sexual infidelity, still to this very day, are living healthy and happy lives because God is the God of restoration.

I was once asked by a new convert who was also a newlywed, "If infidelity had taken place in a marriage, can the couple still stay together?" He wanted to know God's take on such a delicate matter. I'm not sure if he and his wife were experiencing infidelity or not, but I told him it was a personal decision between the husband, the wife, and God. I assured him that if the couple were willing to believe in God for restoration, God would agree with their desires, and God would work with such a couple to restore the marriage covenant that had been broken. No one should ever step into a covenant marital relationship and *tell someone* to divorce their mates for infidelity.

Though unfaithfulness rips at the very heart and soul of one or both spouses, it's too much of a personal matter and a personal decision for a third party to give their advice or opinion. The most an outsider or a third party should do with such a person or couple is to provide them with the Word of God, let them pray about it, and decide for themselves which action to take. Again, that decision should be sought between the couple and God alone.

Abandonment

According to the Word of God, Abandonment is another reason God allows an out in a marriage. The Apostle Paul himself lets us know that "Abandonment" is an option that is allowed for getting a divorce and dissolving a marriage.

In 1 Corinthians chapter 7, the Apostle Paul is teaching concerning marriage, amongst other things. He starts by talking about sexual immorality and how it's not good for a man to touch a woman he's not married to, or a woman who he is not in a covenant relationship with. He talks about every man having his own wife and the wife having her own husband. He then talks about how husbands and wives should perform sexual duties because their bodies are not their own. Therefore, they shouldn't defraud one another sexually. In *1 Corinthians 7:7–8*, he's letting the reader know how he wished that all people were like him in having the "Gift of singleness" so they may wholeheartedly devote themselves to God without any hindrances. Notice here that the Apostle Paul lets us know this *is his desire,* and not God's commandments. Then he says in *1 Corinthians 7:9, "But if they do not have [sufficient] self-control, they should marry; for it is better to marry than to burn* with passion." When we get to *1 Corinthians 7:10–15, it says, "But to the married [believers] I give instructions — not I, but the Lord — that the wife is not to separate from her husband, (but even if she does leave him, let her remain single or else be reconciled to her husband) and that the husband should not leave his wife. To the rest, I declare — I, not the Lord [since Jesus did not discuss this] — that if any [believing] brother has a wife who does not believe [in Christ], and she consents to live with him, he must not leave her. And if any [believing] woman has an unbelieving husband, and he consents to live with her, she must not leave him. For the unbelieving husband is sanctified [that is, he receives the blessings granted] through his*

[Christian] wife, and the unbelieving wife is sanctified through her believing husband. Otherwise, your children would be [ceremonially] unclean, but as it is they are holy. But if the unbelieving partner leaves, let him leave. In such cases, the [remaining] brother or sister is not [spiritually or morally] bound. But God has called us to peace." (AMP)

1 Corinthians 7:15, the Bible says, *"If the unbelieving partner chooses to leave their spouse, let them leave."* However, the Bible says the believing spouse should not leave the unbelieving spouse. Again, if the unbelieving spouse leaves, that's called "abandonment." In this case, God will not hold the believing partner accountable for the divorce if the unbelieving partner chooses to leave and abandons the marriage covenant. The believing partner is then free to get married again, prayerfully, to another believer. Consequently, the Bible says if the unbelieving partner chooses to stay married, the believing partner must not leave or try to find a way out. The believing partner has an opportunity to be used by God to draw the unbelieving partner into a relationship with Christ. The Bible tells us the unbelieving spouse is sanctified by the believing spouse.

Separations

In *1 Corinthians 7:10–11*, *"But to the married [believers] I give instructions — not I, but the Lord — that the wife is not to separate from her husband, (but even if she does leave him, let her remain single or else be reconciled to her husband) and that the husband should not leave his wife."*

The Bible tells us that the wife should not depart or separate from her husband. And if she does separate from him, or vice versa, the separation should result in the couple possibly coming back together again at the appropriate time. Sometimes, a therapeutic separation is necessary for couples to come to the end of themselves. There are times when space is needed in order to get one or both spouses to the place of realizing what is most important during the time of separation. Separation can sometimes be very instrumental in helping couples reflect and remember why they fell in love in the first place. It should be a time to allow God to individually deal with the hearts of each spouse and a time for God to speak to them concerning their marriage. Separation is not a time for a spouse to start dating other people. Again, the will of God is for that couple to come back together again unless they have been given an out based upon the Word of God. Something that is very important to mention is when it comes down to desiring divorce, if at all possible, separations should at least be considered first, before a couple starts thinking about getting a divorce. I'm giving you something to think about here because, once again, God is able to do all things but fail!

Abuse In Marriage

Another very important topic I must discuss is cases in marital relationships where abuse is present. For the record, I would like to state that I am not a social worker. I do not have any certifications or degrees in psychology; therefore, I am not giving professional advice here. I must let you know that no type of abuse is ever considered acceptable in a marriage. It is not the will of God for any person to be verbally abused; emotionally abused; mentally, sexually, or physically abused. Any type of abuse is very damaging and destructive in a marriage, and counseling should most definitely be sought for abuse of any kind in a marriage relationship.

Some individuals believe that verbal, mental, sexual, or emotional abuse is acceptable in a marriage, simply because the abuser feels like they didn't physically strike their mate. Any type of abuse is still abuse and it is not God's will in marriage. So, even though other types of abuse are just as much damaging as physical abuse, I want to speak about physical abuse that might be taking place in your marriage. If the truth is told, physical abuse isn't only occurring in the marriages of non-believers, but it is just as prevalent in the marriages of born-again believers. It takes place in marriages and in the lives of people who genuinely love the Lord. I believe there is too much silence concerning the subject of abuse in Christian marriages. There comes a time in every abusive marriage when what is done in the dark will eventually come to light somewhere along the way. The sad part about it is, on many occasions, it makes its way to the light too late. There have been too many times when it comes to light after someone has been beaten to death.

The word "abuse" comes from two words which are "Abnormal Use." Anytime abuse is present, something is being done that was not the original use for which it was intended or created. It means that it's been used abnormally. God never intended nor advocated abuse to take place in a marriage. It does not matter who you are, and it doesn't matter what title you carry. Abuse is a sin, and it is frowned upon by God. There are also cases where men are abused in marriages as well. However, statistics show that women are far more victims of abuse than men.

If you are in an abusive marriage or even an abusive relationship, I'd first like to say to the one who is being abused that it is not your fault. There is absolutely nothing that you can possibly do to warrant that kind of behavior. There is nothing you can do to be the recipient of abuse, regardless of who is doing the abuse. I say that because too many victims of abuse are made to believe that they deserve to be abused for whatever reason.

If you are being physically abused, you must remove yourself from the home to a safe environment, while you and your mate seek the help that is so desperately needed. If the abuser refuses to seek help, I encourage you to still seek help for yourself. Never stay in a hostile and abusive environment, regardless of how much you love your abuser. I once heard someone ask, "When do I know that it's time to leave in instances of mental abuse, verbal abuse, or emotional abuse?" And, the answer came back, "When the price for the abuse is too much for you to pay." I believe there should not be a price tag that anyone should have to pay when it comes down to abuse. Any price is too much to pay for the psychological damage that takes place. Abuse is detrimental to a relationship. Again, I am not a professional in this matter, but I implore you not to take these abusive situations lightly. Seek God's face, pray and ask God to lead you in how you should respond. If God leads you to remove yourself for a specified time, for a season, or for good, I encourage you to obey the voice of God. Your very life might depend upon it! As I have already stated, many victims of abuse have decided to stay out of fear or for lack of not having anywhere to go. Other possible reasons for staying in an abusive relationship consist of trying to protect the abusive partner or spouse's reputation, not wanting the abuser to possibly do jail time, fear of losing the relationship, to simply suffering from the embarrassment of not wanting family members and friends to know of their present state. Many of these abused victims have paid a tremendous price for staying. Again, many of them have paid with their lives. I believe it is worth mentioning again, that if you are a victim of abuse, remove yourself from the abusive environment and from the abuser and seek the help of trained professionals or your pastor. Whatever you do, don't keep silent when physical abuse is taking place in your marriage. When it comes down to other types of abuse, I personally cannot tell you when or how long you should accept the behavior of the abuser, but it is my prayer that you are fervently seeking God.

If you are the abuser, I would like to say that the Lord loves you dearly. Abuse is not, nor will it ever be the Will of God. I encourage you to seek professional help so that God's healing power can come in and do what only God is able to do. God is a healing God. Therefore, do not allow the spirit of pride and embarrassment to keep you from getting the help that is so desperately needed in your life and in your relationship. The first step to receiving healing is admitting that you are challenged. No one can ever quit what they are not willing to admit. I implore you to seek the face of God.

The Finality of Divorce

As I stated earlier, when it comes down to ending a marriage, divorce is never a part of the will of God for a couple. According to God's Word, God allowed Moses to permit divorce because of the hardness of their hearts. It was never a part of God's original plan. Somewhere along the way, most or all marriages end in divorce due to the hardness of an individual's heart.

Since divorce can be so final, it is imperative that we are cautious not to hurry the process of divorce along without consulting and hearing from God first. Even though God does allow divorce, God is not a fan of divorce. In the eyes of God, marriage is considered to be good. Everything that God made or created, He called Good — even marriage! In *Genesis 2:18, The LORD God also said, "It is NOT GOOD for the man to be alone. I will make for him a suitable helper."* (paraphrased) If God said that it wasn't good for man to be alone, it is evident that God considers the marriage covenant to be good.

No-Fault Divorce

What a Christian couple should desperately strive for is not to be caught in or involved in "A No-Fault Divorce!" In legal terms, many states allow a "No-Fault Divorce" to take place to dissolve a marriage. The courts enable this type of divorce so the couple can end their marriage without doing what most would call "Airing their dirty laundry." It's a divorce that couples get based upon them declaring that they have "Irreconcilable Differences." In short, they want out!

However, Dr. Tony Evans states that a "No-Fault Divorce" is the kind of divorce that has no real merits, and it's a divorce that is not biblically based. In other words, you have no real justifications for wanting out. All you know is that you have reached the breaking point, or you have reached the point of no return, and you want out! PERIOD! I would admonish you to make sure that what you are calling "Irreconcilable Differences" is based upon the Word of God and not solely upon untamed feelings and emotions. Don't angrily move ahead of God with a divorce out of hurt and emotional wounds and scars. "Out," will never be an option to get a divorce just because your spouse has made you mad one too many times or because your frustration level is at an all-time high. That is considered to be "A No-Fault Divorce."

Furthermore, God does not allow divorce because the husband refuses to love the wife as Christ loves the church and because the wife does not respect her husband as God commanded her to do so. I know this can be a hard word for every married couple to digest, but God does not allow divorce because a couple can't seem to get along anymore, or because they are just downright tired of the arguments, strife, and division. Trust me. I get that. However, that's still "Irreconcilable Differences." Many couples have called it quit for that very reason. I know this isn't sitting well with some of you. But, God would much rather for a couple to come to the end of themselves and begin operating in the pure, unadulterated Word of God. He would much rather us to die to ourselves. I want you to rest assured that this word is in no way to bring condemnation upon those who have taken that route for reasons that were not based upon God's Word. God does not condemn you, nor do I. Marriage is not easy. For many, it is and can be a gut-wrenching experience trying to become one.

I, too, know the pain of being emotionally wounded in marriage. My heart has been indescribably scared more times than I care to count as I experienced and wrestled with the fear of wondering if it will ever be repaired or restored again. I have literally experienced my very soul aching from the difficulties of the trials and tribulations associated with marriage.

I'm not sure how many of you have ever experienced an aching soul. My very soul has ached at times. And I know that there will be times that we will need to be restored again, simply because we are two imperfect people who I believe are perfect for one another. My encouragement to you is to always remember that God is a mender of broken hearts, and He is the lifter-up of our heads. God has mended my heart what seems to be thousands of times, but each time, I waited for Him. Sometimes, I had to wait for Him alone, crying in a hotel room. Sometimes I had to wait for Him in the bed of one of my girlfriends. Other times, I waited by my sister's house in another state and sometimes in the spare bedroom. *Isaiah 40:31 tells us, "But those who wait for the LORD [who expect, look for, and hope in Him] Will gain new strength and renew their power; They will lift up their wings [and rise up close to God] like eagles [rising toward the sun]; They will run and now become weary, They will walk and not grow tired."* (AMP)

I can tell you that the enemy literally thought at times that he hit us so far below the belt that we would never recover from the blow. Other times, he believed that he left us for dead. It was only because of the love of God, the grace of God, and the power of the Holy Spirit that helped us to keep getting back up again. I have personally waited for God during times of conflict. I gave God the time and the space to do what only He is capable of doing in my life. Even in the midst of all that pain, God never told me to quit or to get a divorce. He never gave me an exit plan, off-ramp, or a plan B. He never gave me an exit strategy that involved me quitting because I was too weary of moving forward. That's my testimony. I realize and understand that it might not be your testimony. God knows. God understands that there are some instances when one or both spouses have broken the marriage covenant based upon God's Word, and the marriage is most definitely irreparable. In this case, there has been a breach of the marriage covenant. There will be some instances in the marital relationship where divorce is, unfortunately, the only thing left to do. God fully understands that even to the breaking of His heart.

I know every situation is different, but the faithfulness of God and the Word of God will always remain the same. Wherever you are right now in dealing with your marriage — wait for the LORD to lead you and guide you, and He will do just that because He is a faithful God. He shall renew your strength.

Discussing the topic of "When Out Isn't an Option," based upon God's Word, can be one that is vast and very far-reaching. Therefore, I do not have the time or space to speak to all the intricacies concerning the subject matter.

Hopefully, what was shared with you gave you more insight as it relates to the will of God when it comes down to dissolving a marriage.

Closing Thoughts & Comments

As I share with you my last testimony and reiterate some points concerning this book, I want you to know that I have been very prayerful as I wrote this entire book. I have asked the Holy Spirit to download the book into my spirit so when the reader scrolls through the pages, the anointing of God would destroy yokes. I have prayed and asked God to touch struggling marriages. I have asked God to be a roadblock to those who are headed toward a "No-Fault Divorce." I'm praying that you will hear my heart here. I believe that the Spirit of God led me to write this book because God knew I did not want to waste my pain. I wrote it because throughout the years, there were many times the adversary used my pain to tell me that I was not qualified enough to write on this topic. He told me that my marriage would not stand the test of time to

IS OUT EVER AN OPTION?

advise or to encourage others to stand, when my standing seemed to be giving way and faltering.

While I have never been divorced, I can recall the plenty of times when Shawn and I were separated and divided as a couple. Separation, strife, and division within itself have always been very draining to our well-being, naturally and spiritually so. It really didn't matter who was right or who was wrong. Separation always causes both of us to feel spiritually sick from strife and division. The reason is we are one, and our souls have been joined and connected together by God. Again, the pain we both have endured throughout the course of our marriage has caused me, at times, to rethink my marriage vows. If I could be totally transparent here, there were times when the pain of being married caused me to think about an escape route, but God never gave me one based on my own circumstances and based upon His Word.

Have you ever wondered why God is more concerned about *being reconciled* than He is about who's right or who's wrong? It's because strife and division can become detrimental to a marriage. It's also because God is a God of love. We are most like God when we're willing to love like God.

Over the span of sixteen years, when I first began to put pen to paper, I told God countless times that I was not writing this book. I was trapped and immobilized by fear. God also let me know that the delay was also in His perfect will and His perfect timing. God allowed me to know throughout this writing process, He was allowing me to go through many hardships so I could use my experiences to help somebody else. He was in the process of giving me more valuable content in the form of what some might call trouble, but what He calls experience. I had to go through in order to come out on the other side to tell you the story of how I made it over! Not only that, but God so gingerly and lovingly had to allow me to come to terms with the fact that He wasn't giving me an out for the things the enemy told me were an out in marriage. Did you catch that? There have been countless times in my thirty-one-year marriage journey that I honestly thought we weren't going to make it because it seemed as if we had crossed the point of no return. All I can say to you is God is a faithful God and He is worthy to be praised!

Well, my friend, we have come to the end of our journey together. My prayer is that even if a divorce is warranted based upon the Word of God, seek God's face and allow God to move in the situation the way He desires to move. Don't be too hasty with your decisions or your actions. Never discredit what I call "THE GOD FACTOR." That means never underestimate what the omnipotent power of God can do in you, for you, or through you!

Above all, make sure that you are not making a permanent decision based on temporary circumstances. God is able to speak to dead situations and cause them to live again. He is able to give you beauty for ashes. Therefore, always allow God to lead and guide you into all truth. I encourage you to be open to hearing the voice of God more than you are attending to the voice of man, including you. I pray that you will always allow peace to be your umpire.

I believe it is worth mentioning again that even if you get a "No-Fault Divorce," I want you to know that God still loves you dearly. God is a forgiving God, and divorce is not the unpardonable sin. I want you to know that there isn't anything we can do to separate us from the love of God. *Romans 8:1* says, *"Therefore there is now no condemnation [no guilty verdict, no punishment] for those who are in Christ Jesus [who believe in Him as personal Lord and Savior]."* (AMP) Again, Jesus does not condemn you, and neither do I.

I want to let you know that to this very day, I love my husband with all of my heart, and he loves me as well. We make a pretty good team. We have a lot of history together, and I simply cannot imagine living my life without him. Though there aren't a host of guarantees in life outside of God's Word, I certainly continue to pray that our marriage will continue to stand the test of time. I continue to pray that we will forever be yoked together in the Spirit. And I will continue to pray that we will always be overcomers in our marriage. I believe if God did it for us and continues to be that third strand that helps us not easily to be broken, He will also do the same for you! He's a keeping God. He is our sustenance. He will keep those things that we commit to Him for safekeeping. And that includes our marriage.

Finally, I say to you that marriage is HAR, but God is able to do all things but fail. *Luke 18:27* says, *"What is impossible with man is possible with God."* (NIV) He is the God of Impossibilities! So, I admonish you that before you make the final decision to dissolve your marriage, make sure you are consulting God above all else. Continue to hold fast to the profession of your faith. Don't get weary in well-doing. Put in the laborious work to stay together if God hasn't given you an off-ramp in marriage. Even though *"Out Is an Option"* in marriage, always remember that in the eyes of God, "Marriage Should Be for Keeps!" I love you!

PRAYER: Father God in Heaven. I pray for all of those who have read this book. Father God, my prayer is that You would always allow them to know that You are with them. You promised us in Your Word that You would never leave us or forsake us. You have given us the invitation to come boldly before the throne of grace that we may obtain mercy and find grace to help in times of trouble and in times of need. Help us Lord, in all of our decisions and in all of life's endeavors. Touch our families, God, and strengthen us as only You can. Touch our relationships. Touch those of us who are married and help us to stand. God, touch those who are significantly struggling in their marriages. Help us to know what it means to be long-suffering and what it means to walk in love and to walk in forgiveness. Help us to be reminded of what the God-kind of love looks like, while giving us the willingness to display it in our marriages. Touch every engaged couple, as well as couples who are contemplating divorce. Be with them, Lord. Speak ever-so-loudly to them. Dear heavenly Father, I'm also lifting up in prayer those who have already gone through the process of divorce. Let them know how you love them so dearly. Let them know that they are not a failure because there's no failure in You! Heal the hearts of those who stand in need of healing. Bring deliverance to those who need to be rescued. Father God, strengthen us all individually and collectively. Let us constantly be reminded of the victory that You have already given us through the shed blood of Jesus Christ. God, most of all, let us all be reminded that You have called us to peace! Therefore, I ask all these things in Jesus' Name! And this is my prayer. Amen!

Over thirty-two years ago, this handsome man of God went on a quest, looking for me to make me his bride. Proverbs 18:22 says, "He who finds a wife finds a good thing and obtains favor from the LORD!" I am so blessed by God to be his "Good Thing!"

While endeavoring to have a solid and healthy marriage, we must learn how to love with the God-kind of love. I call it the 1st Corinthians 13-kind of love. It's the kind of love that is patient. It's the kind of love that endures all things, hopes all things, and believes all things. Love is not easily angered or agitated; it is willing to forgive and suffer long. Love covers and throws a veil over a multitude of sins. "So, now faith, hope, and love abide, these three, but the greatest of these is love!"

About the Author

Adriene Conner is an avid reader. In her spare time, it's not unusual to find her reading two to three books at a time. Some of her favorite pastimes are watching good movies, going out to eat, spending time with family, or having quiet time alone. One of her greatest and most passionate desires in life is studying and sharing the Word of God.

She is one of the founding Pastors of Perfecting the Saints Teaching Ministry. She along with her husband teaches a weekly bible study called "FRESH FIRE," where they share God's Word, as a way of helping the people of God live their best lives. She has been called by God to help others walk in victory as they apply the principles of God's Word to their lives.

Adriene resides in Slidell, Louisiana. She was born and raised in New Orleans, LA, where she spent the majority of her life, before moving to Slidell, LA. She is a licensed Life Insurance Broker who sells final expense insurance plans. She believes having the "Assurance" of "Insurance" goes a long way!

She is married to Elder Shawn C. Conner. They have been married for over 31 years. Together, they have two handsome sons named Caleb and Joshua Conner, who they affectionate call "The Faith Team." They have also been blessed with a beautiful granddaughter named Jayde, whom they love with all of their hearts.

To connect with Adriene Conner, visit:

Facebook @ Adriene Conner

Instagram @ Adrieneconnerministries

Adrieneconner.com

Info@Adrieneconner.com

www.ingramcontent.com/pod-product-compliance
Lightning Source LLC
Chambersburg PA
CBHW050450270326
41927CB00009B/1675